UNSTOPPABLE

PRAISE

Though He Slay Me, Yet Will I Hope in Him

MYRLANDE JOSEPH

About the Book

This book of poetry was written under the inspiration of the Holy Spirit while I was in God's presence, praising and thanking Him in the midst of my pain and despair during a five-year period in which I found myself stuck with a master's degree, yet jobless with no income. I had lost my car and my identity. I had received a Section 8 voucher six months after completing my degree while my son and I were without a place to call home, only to lose it two years later. So we hit rock bottom, crashing on friends' couches and floors, sleeping in car, being rejected left and right by employers, and in a state of depression, feeling forsaken, abandoned, embarrassed, humiliated, overlooked, judged, ashamed, lonely, confused, and lost, with little or no help from those who had capacities at the time to help me.

Many people had given me false hope and deaf ears. It was a very difficult and depressed time for me to see myself, at my age with a college degree and a grown son, crashing at other people's homes with no job. I felt embarrassed! I tried everything to break free from my dead-end situations, but I could not get out of them. No degrees, no set of skills, nor the many prayers could get me out. God was silent for whatever reason. Can you relate?

However, though I couldn't understand the reason for my pains and sufferings or the silence from God, I made up my mind to give Him praise and worship Him. I counted my blessings that it could have been a lot worse. Like Job, I thought, "Though he slay me, yet will I hope in Him" (Job 13:15). And nothing was going to stop me from praising and thanking my God, even at times when I would feel so weak and broken and wanted to give up in life. Truly, what mattered most was that I had His breath in me to worship Him.

It was while I was in His presence, praising and thanking Him for His breath, goodness, and provisions in my life, that the Holy Spirit would drop a poem in my spirit to write. Soon I found myself writing a poem almost every day about trials and struggles I had faced over the years, issues of life, those who the media reported had committed suicide, etc. Most of these poems were inspired by the Holy Scriptures while I was praising and meditating on the Word of God.

In those years, all I had going for me were my praise, worship, and writing. One of my friends once said, "The things you are experiencing in life should have led you into a mental institution, but instead you have not stopped praising God in the midst of your storms." We live in a world in which we face all kinds of trials, and we can easily feel discouraged, become angry with God, lose our joy and passion for praise, or even give up on God. Some life challenges can be so overwhelming that the last thing I would want to do in those circumstances is give praise to God. But thanks be to God for giving me a garment of praise where I always find myself in His presence—blessing His name through my trials. The good news is that same garment is available for you today, and it's not too late for you to get your passion back and praise Him. As David says, "I will extol the LORD at all times; his praise will always be on my lips" (Psalm 34:1).

God had a plan and purpose for my pains and sufferings. Most importantly, He had good reasons for the silence. It's not that He couldn't get me out of my situation and deliver me as you will soon read the testimonies of Him revealing Himself to me and answering my prayers over and over in my upcoming book, *Don't Be Afraid To Pray.* There are times, like Job, when we do not know why God is silent or why we are suffering.

Who would have thought this poetry book would come from pain and despair? No matter what you're experiencing in life, don't give up on God or your praise of Him. God is not yet done with you. He has a plan for your life. Keep praising Him in the midst of your storms. He deserves our praise at all times—not just when everything is going well for us, but also in bad times.

My prayer for you is that these poems will encourage you while you are waiting on God to reveal Himself to you.

Acknowledgment

Thank you, Lord, for this poetry book You have birthed in me through my pains and sufferings. And thank you for how You had kept me in perfect peace to write it under the inspiration of the Holy Spirit when all hell had broken loose in my life. Truly, in all things, you work for the good of those who love You and who have been called according to Your purpose. Now I see that my sufferings were not in vain and You had a plan and purpose for them. As always, may Your name be praised, magnified, and glorified through me.

Contents

Dedication

This poetry book is written to inspire and encourage those who are going through a crisis to not give up on God or your praise. I want you to know that you are not alone and that others have been where you are. You may not know or understand the reason for your sufferings; however, I believe that God has a plan and a purpose for them.

Poems by Category

Praise and Worship

I Wonder

I Have You

All Your Ways

It Doesn't Matter

I Praise You

That Name

I Give You Praise

Why Not Come?

Paradise

I Must Give Them Back

Why One Day?

I Wonder

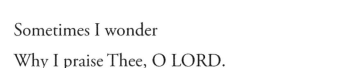

Sometimes I wonder

Why I praise Thee, O LORD.

I wonder why I want to praise You

From the moment I am awake,

When I could just stay in bed

And dwell on my past and present condition,

When I could just stay in bed

Feeling sorry for me.

I wonder why Your praise

Is always on my lips

And the desire to worship You in the morning

Is so strong.

Tell me, why do I worship Thee, O LORD?

Could it be You blessed me

With a house with my name on it,

Or I woke up with a husband next to me?

It couldn't be.

The couch and pillows held me last night.

So why do I worship Thee, then?

Why bless Your name

From the moment I am awake?

Why wake up singing praises to You

When I could just weep all day long?

Is it because my car is parked out there?

From what I can remember,

Last time I had one was four years ago.

In fact, I Ubered yesterday.

Okay. Well, tell me why I worship Thee?

Why praise You from the moment I am awake?

Why shout Hallelujah to You

When I could just cry out, "Help me!!

I got it—my dreams have come to pass.

You fulfilled the desires of my heart.

I am now living on purpose.

Unfortunately, the desires were just there a minute ago,

And the dreams are still on my heart.

Nevertheless, the streets are still filled

With homeless and hungry people.

So why do I worship Thee?

Why praise and glorify Your name

When the condition is still the same

And everything is dead in my life?

Why I couldn't get off my bed

Until I praise Thee?

Wait a minute! I think I know why!

You breathed life into me today!

And your Word says,

"Let everything that has breath praise the Lord!"

(Psalm 150:6)

I Have You

It's okay if I don't have it all on this day.

It's okay that I'm still waiting, dreaming,

And hoping to see Your glory in my life.

It's okay that it has been over two decades

Since I've been waiting for the appointed time,

Waiting for the promises to fulfill,

Waiting for the dreams to come to pass.

Truly, none of these things matter.

What matters most is that I have Your breath in me

To worship you day and night

And glorify Your name above all names.

It's okay that the condition is still the same

And that I am still dreaming and hoping,

Waiting to see Your glory manifest in my life,

Waiting to see myself before great men,
Waiting to see Your name glorified in my life.
Yet, Lord, I will still praise You
And magnify Your holy name.

Truly, none of these things matter.
The delay is too small
To keep me from praising You.
All the storms of life are too small
To stop me from praising You.
The rejections and snubs are too small
To keep me from glorifying Your name.
The unfulfilled dreams are too small
To stop me from exalting You.
The desires are too small
To impede me from blessing You.
My purpose, my destiny are too small
To stop me from magnifying Your name.

So, it's okay
If I don't have it all on this day.
It's okay

That I am still waiting on You.

It's okay

That the condition and situation are still the same.

It's okay.

I will worship You anyway,

Lord.

For I am convinced

That neither a car,

A home,

A husband,

Wealth,

Possessions,

Delays,

Unanswered prayers,

Or unfulfilled dreams

Will be able to stop me

From blessing Your name.

So, it's okay.

I may not have it all today.

I may still wait

For the dreams to come to pass

I may still wait

To fulfill my destiny.

But I have You, Lord.

I have You, Lord,

I have You.

You are still worth my praise.

What matters most

Is that I have You.

If I have You,

I have everything in You.

So, it's okay

That I'm still waiting

To see the dreams come to pass.

It's okay

That I'm still waiting

To fulfill my destiny.

But I have You, Lord.

I have the gift of life today.

I have the gift of salvation.

I have the gift of the Holy Spirit in me.

I have your angel

That encamps around me day and night,

Your love and mercy

That follow me,

Your divine protection

Over me and my loved ones

So is Your presence

That goes with me everywhere I go.

I may not have it all,

But I have You

If I have You,

I have everything in You.

(Romans 8:38; Psalm 34:7; Psalm 23:6; Exodus 33:15)

All Your Ways

O, how I long each day to shout, "Hallelujah,"

Making sound in Your ear,

Singing fresh and new melodies to You each day,

Praising You and magnifying Your name.

Hallelujah, glory be to Your name, Jesus,

King of kings, and Lord of lords,

The great King over all the earth

Who is perfect in all Your ways.

O God, my Lord, my Salvation,

How I love to praise Your holy name,

Exalt it every day and night!

For You are perfect, faithful,

And gracious in all Your ways.

Indeed, all Your ways

Are loving and faithful toward me.

Therefore, I shout, "Hallelujah!"

To You, my God,

Creator of heaven and earth.

Today, I worship You, O God.

Right in the midst of my storms

I glorify Your name.

O Glory be to Your name,

O God, my salvation,

My deliverer, my way-maker, my provider.

Hallelujah to the Alpha and Omega.

The First and the Last,

The Beginning and the End,

The Great God who is perfect

In all his ways.

(Psalm 136:3; Revelation 19:16, 22:13)

It Doesn't Matter

He whispered, "Are you out of your mind?
Don't you have anything better
To do with your life?
Why still praise Him?
Why shout Hallelujah
When everything remains the same?
Why still bless His name
When everything is upside down in your life
And you're still stuck?"

It doesn't matter, Father of Lies.
I will bless Him in good and bad times.
Forever I will bow down and worship Him,
For He is worthy of praise.
He deserves it day and night,
In good and bad times.

Yes, I know I called and got no answer.

I asked, I did not receive.

I sought, I did not find.

I knocked, the doors did not open.

I stood on the Word, but they didn't come to life.

And yes, my life is filled with rejections.

Again, it doesn't matter, Father of Lies.

I will worship Him anyway,

For my God is not dead!

He is still seated on His holy throne.

My God is not a man, that He should lie.

Indeed, He has a plan for my life,

Plans to give me hope and a future.

So, I will glorify His name,

For He has done wonders before.

He has done great things in the past.

It doesn't matter, Father of Lies.

My soul will bless the Lord

And glorify His holy name.

I may not be where I want to be,

But I am not who I used to be

Twenty-one years ago.

(John 8:44; Psalm 34:1; Matthew 7:7; Numbers 23:19; Psalm 47:8; Jeremiah 29:11)

I Praise You

Yes, Lord, it's true!

Nobody told me to get up this morning and give You praise.

My situation did not encourage me at all to praise You.

In fact, my condition said, "No!"

The flesh said, "No!" and "Can't do it today!"

Meanwhile, my thoughts were all over,

Wondering when You would come to my rescue.

If I had listened to them,

You would not get this praise from me today.

If I had let my emotions control me

When I woke up this morning,

You would not get this praise today.

If I had given in to the flesh,

I would not have praised You

Like I did this morning.

Truly, the flesh was weak

And couldn't seem to let me praise You.

My thoughts, on the other hand,

Couldn't seem to be focus on Your goodness.

As You see, though the flesh was weak,

My spirit was willing.

Though my emotions did all they could to control me,

Your Spirit would not let them.

Again, I did not praise You today

Because my situation changed,

And I am where I want to be in life.

I didn't praise You

Because my prayers were answered

Or I saw the husband next to me

When I woke up today.

I didn't praise You

Because I have wealth, riches, or possessions.

I praised You because I love you,

And I desire to bless Your name

That is above all names.

Nobody, nor my flesh, thoughts, or emotions,

Told me to praise You but Your Spirit.

So, Holy Spirit,

Thank you for enabling me to praise Him today.

(Matthew 26:41; Philippians 2:9)

That Name

I love to praise that name—

His name that is a strong tower.

O, how I love to lift that name up

And exalt it before men,

Blessing it day and night!

Are there other names like His name?

Is there a name more powerful than His name?

Truly, there is no other name like His name.

No other name can save me like that name,

For in that name

I am delivered, healed, and set free.

In that name

I am restored and victorious.

In that name

I am the head, not the tail.

O, how I long to bless that name

Forever and ever,

That name that is the way, the truth, and the life,

And giving it an unstoppable praise,

Forever praised!

Yes, there is power in that name.

There is salvation, healing, deliverance, and restoration.

Surely, I will bless it forever and ever.

I will lift it high,

For that name is a strong tower,

And at the sound of it,

Every knee should bow.

Everyone should confess

That Jesus is Lord.

O, how I love to praise that name, Jesus!

(Proverbs 18:10; Deuteronomy 28:13; John 14:6; Philippians 2:10)

I Give You Praise

Lord, I don't need to be

Where I want to be today

To give You praise.

I don't need to have the job or a home

To give You praise.

I don't need to have a car

To drive to a church building

To give You praise.

My situation doesn't need to turn around

To give You praise.

My condition doesn't need to change

To give You praise.

I will give You praise right where I am,

In the silence,

In my dead situation,

In the confusion,

In the unknown.

Hallelujah, glory be to Your name, Jesus,

My Lord, my salvation!

O God of Abraham, Isaac, and Jacob,

I give You praise

Right in the middle of the storm.

O God of deliverance, God of breakthrough,

I give You praise

Right in the midst of the darkest season.

You, O Lord,

Who is an ever-present help in trouble,

Strong and mighty in battles,

I give You praise on this day!

(Psalm 24:8, 46:1)

Why Not Come?

Aren't you tired of running around,

Talking about your problems,

Looking for someone to hear your cry,

Someone to help and comfort you,

Someone to validate you,

Someone to accept you for you,

Someone to know your name?

Why not come and worship Him?

Why not come and glorify Him with me?

The one and only Lord,

The one who calls you by name,

The one who's close to the broken-hearted

And has saved those who are crushed in spirit,

The one whose eyes are on the righteous

And whose ears are attentive to their cries.

Aren't you tired of doing the usual

Day after day and night after night?

Why waste your entire day watching the news,

Listening to worldly views and sad songs,

Dwelling on your past mistakes,

Thinking of what you should have said or done?

When yesterday is gone,

When He created you to worship Him,

When in his presence

There is fullness of joy.

Why not come out of your comfort zone,

Out of your misery and sad self, and worship Him?

Why not come and magnify the Lord with me?

For great is His name and most worthy of praise!

So come, let us worship Him together!

(Psalm 16:11, 34:18–19, 145:3)

Paradise

I'm wondering if it is just me

Dreaming of this day,

This day I will be with Him forever.

I'm wondering if there's anyone else like me out there

Dreaming of this day,

Envisioning what it's going to be like,

Looking forward to seeing Him.

I'm wondering if there's anyone else out there

Who can't wait to bless His name forever

In paradise?

O, how I long to see my King,

How I long to worship Him for eternity,

My Lord and my salvation,

The one who reigns forever and ever!

For I was born to worship Him.

I was chosen for this very purpose
To worship Him in spirit with the angels
Forever and ever.

For paradise is what I dream of.
Paradise is what I desire.
Nothing else matters
But to be with Him for eternity,
Worshiping Him with the angels,
Blessing Him forever and ever,
Exalting Him for ever and ever,
Glorifying His name for ever and ever,
Magnifying His name forever and ever.
All I want, all I desire
Is to be with Him
In paradise!

I Must Give Them Back

I know, I know

What they said about me.

There's no doubt about them.

Indeed, they are true.

But I can't keep them for me.

I must give them back.

I know, I know

Everyone is talking about them.

The entire world heard about them.

But I can't keep them for me.

I must give them back,

For they do not belong to me,

Nor do they belong to another

Or to an idol.

Sorry, I must give them back
To where they first originated,
To the One who made a way for me.
I must give them back
To where they first manifested
In the heavenly realms,
From the Father, the Giver, the Author,
And the Finisher of my faith.
For in Him I live, move,
And have my being.

So, why keep them
When they are not mine to keep?
Why hold on to them
When they do not belong to me?
Why keep them
When apart from Him I can do nothing?
Did you not hear?
He will not give his glory to another
Or his praise to an idol.

Truly only He deserves the praise, the glory, and the honor.

Therefore, I must give them back to Him—

Not some, but all the praise and glory.

(Hebrews 12:2; Acts 17:28; John 15:5; Isaiah 42:8)

Why One Day?

I think He deserves more than just one day.

I think He should be remembered more often.

I think He should be celebrated more.

Why one day?

Aren't there 365 days in a year?

Why wait 359 days to celebrate Him?

Don't you have breath in you?

I think He's too good and too awesome of a King

To be celebrated just one day.

You mean to tell me,

All He deserves is just one day?

His birth can only be remembered on that day,

A day when you look around you,

It has nothing to do with Him,

Barely mention His name,

And barely acknowledge Him,

Not after all He has done for you and me,

Being separated from His Father,

Born in a manger,

Was humiliated,

Wrongly accused,

Beaten, crucified, and carried our cross,

Died and rose on the third day.

Now because He lives

And we, too, live.

I think He should be celebrated more often.

I think He should be remembered more often.

Why one day?

Aren't there 365 days in a year?

Don't you think He deserves to be celebrated more,

To be remembered more often?

I mean, I can understand

If you were indeed celebrating Him the entire day

Or if He was your priority and focus.

In fact, you're not even thinking of Him.

Your action alone says it all.

It's obvious it hasn't been about Him;

It's been about your business.

He's too awesome and too good of a Lord

To be remembered one day out of 365 days.

I think He's worthy to be celebrated more often.

I think He's worthy to be praised every day—

Not just one day,

But three hundred sixty-five days!

(Luke 21:6–7; 1 Corinthians 15:4; John 14:19)

Homelessness

I Want To Go Home

Rich in Faith

The Station

I Know

I Want to Go Home

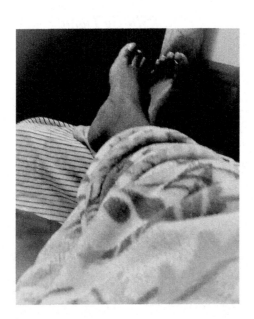

I want to go home to a place

Where I don't have to rush to get up from where I lay

And stay there, worshipping Him all day long,

A place where I can just stay in bed

And reflect on my entire life

And cry out loud to God,

A place I can call home

Where I am free to do whatever I want.

Lord, I want to go home to that place again,

That place I once have called home

That was taken from me suddenly.

When can I go there again?

For You said in Your Word,

"With deep compassion I will bring you back."

Please, Lord, take me home one more time.

I want to go home.

Have mercy on me, God,

For I have no one who can take me there with deep compassion,

And I can't do it on my own, Lord.

My zero income will not permit me to do so.

But You, O Lord, are not limited by anything.

God of restoration, God of deliverance,

I want to go home to the place when I was once free.

(Isaiah 54:7)

Rich in Faith

Castle Self Storage, Braintree, MA

I may not have a home now,

I may not have wealth, possessions, or status,

But one thing I know:

I am rich!

I know my condition tells you something else.

The situation says, 'Poverty.'

Indeed, I am a wealthy woman—

Not with possessions, but rich in faith!

What more can I ask for

When He is everything I am—

My Glory! My Righteousness! My Shield! My Rock!

When He is everything I have going on for me—

My Provider! My help! My Healer! My Protector! My

Defense! My Refuge!

I may not look like one in your definition of prosperity.

I may not look like one in your definition of success.

My condition may speak louder

Than the very word coming out of my mouth:

That I am rich.

But believe me when I say,

I am rich!

For what more can I ask for

When He is everything I want—

My Joy! My Peace! My Strength! My Strong Tower!

What more can I ask for

When in Him I live, move, and have my being?

In Him I'm healed, delivered, and set free.

I may not look like the typical wealthy woman,

But if you would look at the above list,

You would indeed see that I am rich.

You would see that no amount of money can buy me

His divine healing,

His divine protection,

His divine provision.

No amount of money can buy me His peace,

His peace that passes all understanding,

His joy that is my strength.

Indeed, I am rich!

Not with money or fame, but rich in faith!

Faith that comes from hearing His Word.

(Philippians 4:7; Acts 17:28; Nehemiah 8:10; Romans 8:17)

The Station

I did not expect to still be here almost two hours later,

Waiting to be picked up

Just so I could go to sleep.

I am cold, sleepy, and hungry.

I wonder what I've done to be stuck at this station,

Waiting to be picked up,

Waiting to be in a warm place.

I am cold, sleepy and hungry,

But I'm stuck at a station.

I wonder when this struggle will end?

For I want to be set free and delivered from homelessness.

I want to be set free from being unemployed.

I want to be set free from poverty.

Truly, a decision must be made soon about my life.

I can't live this struggle anymore.

I am currently shaken up.

I can barely open my eyes,

Thinking where else I can go from this station.

I am feeling anxious—

All because I did not get enough sleep the night before.

Last night I cried myself to sleep.

Two in the morning I was still up.

I kept on turning and turning,

All because I was uncomfortable.

I wonder what I've done wrong to still be at this station,

Waiting to be picked up,

Waiting to be in a warm place.

I am cold, sleepy, and hungry.

Finally picked up almost two hours later,

I can't seem to get some sleep.

I don't know what to do to get some sleep.

Jesus! I need some sleep to concentrate.

Please deliver me and set me free!

When will be the day I see myself home again?

I want to be set free from homelessness.

I want to be set free from unemployment.

I want to be set free from poverty.

Truly, a decision must be made soon about my life,

For I can't live this struggle anymore.

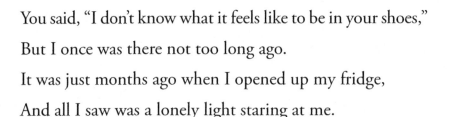

I Know

You said, "I don't know what it feels like to be in your shoes,"
But I once was there not too long ago.
It was just months ago when I opened up my fridge,
And all I saw was a lonely light staring at me.
Trust me, I've been there and lived it.

You said, "I can't relate to you or understand you,"
But I know what it's like to have and not have.
Please don't let the look fool you now.
In fact, I do know what it's like to be without a bed.
It was just yesterday I woke up with my back
Feeling sore from the couch with little sleep.
It was just one night ago when I lay down to sleep
With no one to keep me warm for two decades.
Of course, I know what it's like to be single.

Trust me when I say,

I know the meaning of being lonely

Because recently I reminded God of His Word,

"It's not good for a man to be alone."

I know, I know what it's like to wonder

Where my next meal is going to come from.

I know what it's like to be homeless

And find yourself in random places.

I know, I know what it's like to be humiliated,

Overlooked, forsaken, and rejected.

Trust me when I say I know,

I understand, and I can relate.

So, please don't be fooled by my nice attire.

You have no idea what I've been through.

So, trust me when I say

I know what it's like to be you.

(Genesis 2:18)

Waiting and Giving Up

Life within the Four Walls

I Don't Recall

Why Should I Settle?

Why Now?

Life within the Four Walls

There is no exit for me.

I'm wondering how to exit these walls—

These empty walls that have stared at me for some time now.

I want to break free from them today

And see what's on the other side of them.

I want to escape from these walls,

But I don't know how or who to call

To exit me out.

Truly, I want to escape from these walls—

These empty walls I have been staring at for some time now.

I want to escape this awful shame,

This feeling of being without a job

And finding myself with nowhere to go

But to stare at these walls.

It has been some time now

Since I have been looking at these walls

With nothing exciting about them.

My mind is overwhelmed with so many thoughts.

How I wish I had a wealthy relative living in a different

part of the world,

Like an aunt, uncle, grandparent, sister, or brother I could

just call to come and rescue me from these four walls.

How I wish I had a father

Who could provide for me.

I don't know what to do,

Which exit to take,

Who besides God to call to come and rescue me.

Truly, I can't rely on any man,

For many have given me false hopes

And never fulfilled their promises to me.

Who would have thought, at my age,

Today I would still be in this condition,

Stuck and unable to move forward?

I know I have sinned and fallen short of the glory of God.

But I don't know which one I am being punished for.

I don't know which one I have suffered for.

Then again, maybe I am not being punished for any of them.

Maybe I'm just like Job, where God is asking Satan,

"Do you consider my servant Myrlande?"

Or maybe God is up to something

And getting ready to blow some minds

As He told me not too long ago.

Therefore, I will wait on Him

And watch Him make a way for me

To exit these prison walls.

(Romans 3:23; Job 1:8)

I Don't Recall

Lord, it has been some time

Since You brought change in my condition,

Since I last saw Your glory

And tasted Your goodness.

Lord, it has been some time

Since I saw You move,

Since I last experienced Your miracle power.

I don't recall You ever being this late.

I don't recall You taking so long

To come to my rescue

And not revealing yourself to me,

Not turning my situation.

You have always been near to me

When I call Your name,

But it has been some time,

Since I am still in the same condition

With no one to come to my rescue.

Yes, Lord, it has been some time

Since You last touched me,

Since You last gave me a word

And showed Yourself in my life.

For some time now

I have been on the lookout,

Hoping the phone will ring with good news,

Hoping my email will fill with good news.

It has been some time

Since I've experienced a shift from You,

A breakthrough

And an exodus

Like that of the Israelites.

Truly, God,

I don't recall You ever being this late.

I don't recall You ever being slow to answer.

You have always been present in my trouble

When I called upon You.

You have always been faithful to me,

But it has been awhile now

Since I saw an open door

Or entered a new season,

Since I last saw Your glory shine upon me

And experienced Your miracle power.

From what I can remember,

You have always been a present help in my trouble,

Able to save and deliver me.

Your ears have always been attentive to my cry

And have always turned my mourning into dancing.

Now, since I don't understand

The reason for this delay,

Please help me to trust Your timing.

Help me not to lose heart

Or doubt Your ability,

For You have always been faithful to me.

(Psalm 30:11, 34:16, 46:1, 145:18)

Why Should I Settle?

Settle! No!

I refuse to settle!

Believe me, it's too late for that,

When I know the power is within me,

When I know the earth is His and everything in it,

The world and all who live in it.

Why should I settle

When I have already experienced His power

And witnessed it in other's lives?

Why should I settle

When His promises are 'yes' and 'amen'?

I think it's a little too late, don't you think?

I think it's a little too late to settle for less.

It wasn't long ago

When I witnessed His glory in someone's life,

When suddenly He turned her situation around
And blessed her with the desire of her heart.

Maybe if I didn't know
He rose on the third day,
Maybe if I didn't know
I serve a big God,
Maybe if I didn't know
He is the God of glory, miracles, and restoration,
Or maybe if I didn't know
All power, wealth, and possessions belong to Him.

Why should I settle
When He has already proven Himself to me?
Believe me, it's too late to settle now.
It's too late to settle for less,
Not when I know
Nothing is impossible with Him,
Not when I remember
From where He had brought me,
Not after I experienced
His healing and resurrection power

In another's life.

So, I refuse to settle,

But to wait on the Lord.

(Psalm 24:1–2, 145:19; 2 Corinthians 1:20)

Why Now?

Why now, soul? Why give up now?

Have you forgotten who He is?

Do you not remember what He has done for me

And from where He has brought me?

Tell me, what's changed about His nature?

It wasn't long ago

When I was testifying about His goodness in my life,

Bragging about the marvelous things

He has done for me.

Why now, soul?

Why feel discouraged within me?

Why want to give up when He is not dead?

It wasn't long ago

When He made a way out of no way for me,

When He shifted things in my favor

And put a smile on my face.

Hear me out, soul,

You will not give up on Him,

For He hasn't given up on me.

So, why give up now?

Last time I checked,

He was the same miracle God

And the same deliverance God.

Is there a mountain He cannot move?

Is there a chain He cannot break?

Is there a condition He cannot change?

Why give up now

When the condition is temporary?

Why now

When He can do immeasurably more

Than we can ask or imagine?

(Ephesians 3:20)

Alone and Forsaken, Helpless, Hopeless

Not Alone

He Won't Let Me Go

The Best Gift

Have Mercy

Help Me

I Miss My Father

Show Me

Not Alone

Don't be fooled by my condition

Where I am stuck

And can't find anybody to come and rescue me.

Don't be fooled by how others have treated me

As if I were some kind of orphan.

Though He seems invisible, I am not alone,

For He lives in me and I in Him.

Please don't let the trials fool you

Into thinking no one cares about me.

He is with me and for me.

He sees all things and knows all things.

He is not surprised by the treatment I receive from others.

He is not surprised by those who turn their backs on me.

He is not surprised by those who judge me or look down

on me.

I am not alone; I am not forsaken.

Though you can't see Him,

His presence works behind the scenes.

Again, don't be fooled by my challenges.

In the midst of my trials, He is there.

In the midst of my loneliness, He is there.

In the midst of my storms, He is there.

In the midst of my sorrows, He is there.

I'm not alone and never will be.

(1 John 4:13)

He Won't Let Me Go

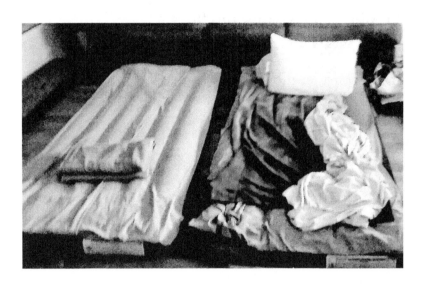

This is not the life I dreamed of after coming to America.

This is not the life I envisioned after college.

I never thought at my age

I would be sleeping at someone else's home

With no source of income.

I never thought at my age

I would still be without companionship.
I never thought at my age I would be without a vehicle.

Oh, how I feel forsaken!
Oh, how I feel ashamed and embarrassed!
Oh, how I feel hopeless and helpless!
All I want to do is escape this life.
I want to escape this life,
But He won't let me go.
I want to leave this world,
But God won't release me.

Could it be He still has a plan for me?
Could it be He is not yet done with me?
Why won't He let me go
When nothing is happening for me?
Does that mean He's not done yet with me?
Could He possibly have a plan for my life?
For I want to escape this life,
But He upholds me with His hands
And refuses to let me go.

What does that mean?

Is He delighted in my way?

This was never the life I envisioned after giving my life to
Him.

This was never the life I dreamed of after graduate school.

I never thought at my age I would jump from one place to
another.

I never thought at my age I would crash at a friend's place.

I don't know if I can handle another day,

Waking up and seeing myself in this condition.

I don't know if I can handle another day,

Seeing myself jobless with no income.

I never thought I would be without a home after college.

I never thought I would be without a paycheck.

O, how I feel left out and forsaken!

O, how I feel abandoned and lonely!

All I want to do is escape this life!

I want to escape,

But He won't let me go.

I want to leave this world,

But God won't release me.

Could it be He is not yet done with me?
Could it be He still has a plan for my life?
Why won't He let me go?
Why won't He let me escape this world
When nothing is happening for me?
Could there still be hope for me after all these years?
Maybe there is
Because He refuses to let me go.
Like Job, "Though he slay me, yet will I hope in him."

(Isaiah 41:10; Job 13:15)

The Best Gift

It has been some time since we've last spoken.

It has been some time since my hand had reached out to yours.

And now you're angry with me

And even said you're done with me.

This is understandable.

Who wouldn't be angry when knowing that

Your relative is living in a land of opportunity,

And yet you're still in the same situation,

The first one to ever achieve a college degree,

And yet you're still experiencing shame, humiliation, and insult?

I completely understand,

Especially when she has the capacity to bring others to this land,

And yet she has forsaken them,

You have every right to say you're done with me.

But hear me out:

You may not have heard from me for a while,

I may not have sent anything to you for some time,

But I've given you something far richer than money or gold,

Interceding for you day and night,

Exercising my faith that comes from hearing God's Word,

Covering you in prayer day and night,

Binding and canceling the assignment of the enemy

Over your life and their lives.

You may not want it,

But the best gift I can give you at the present time

Is prayer.

Money and gold I do not have,

But the best gift I can give you is prayer.

(Romans 10:17; Acts 3:5)

Have Mercy

Lord, have mercy on me,

For I don't know what else to do

Or which way to go anymore.

I ran out of ideas,

I ran out of places to look.

Is this Your will for my life?

Tell me, if it is,

Then I need Your grace to embrace it.

If not, please have mercy on me

Many who once were in my condition

Have moved on with their lives.

I am the only one without an income,

The only one still in prison

And waiting to be set free.

What sin have I committed

That no one has ever done before?

For all have sinned and fallen short of your glory.

And yet, I am the only one left in my condition,

Moving from one place to another.

Though it's not true, I feel forsaken and overlooked.

I understand You show mercy

To whomever You want to show mercy,

But today I am asking You to have mercy on me,

For I've been in this condition for five years.

Please, Lord, have mercy on me

As You have had on others.

You might have a good reason

For holding this blessing from me,

The very thing that can get me out of my situation,

The very blessing that can set me free

From homelessness and poverty,

But it's not easy to still be in the same condition

Day after day and year after year.

So, Lord, have mercy on me

According to Your unfailing love.

(Romans 3:23; Exodus 33:19; Luke 18:38)

Help Me

O Spirit of God, move!

I am stuck and can't find a way out.

I am trapped and can't move forward.

I am lost and can't be found by anyone.

Where else can I go, Spirit of God?

Whom can I call?

Please come to my rescue!

Some probably wonder,

Where is her Helper?

Where is her Counselor?

It's been some time now.

Doesn't she believe in the power of the Holy Spirit?

But where is He?

O Spirit of the Living God,

Spirit of truth, Spirit of fresh and new revelation,

Move quickly, and reveal Yourself to them,

You who reside in me,

You who are not limited by anything,

You who can reveal Yourself to me and lead me the way,

Don't let them question Your ability to help me.

Don't let them doubt Your power that is in me

To accomplish all things and become all things.

So, Holy Spirit, my Advocate, my Comforter,

Move on my behalf on this day!

I Miss My Father

I miss you, Dad!

I miss You with all my heart.

I miss being in Your presence,

Worshiping You and blessing Your name,

Lifting Your name high above all names.

I miss You, Daddy!

Please help me find my way back into Your presence,

Singing praises to You,

Blasting praise and worship music once more.

O how my soul longs for fellowship with my Father!

O how I miss our intimacy!

For once I feel so far from you, Dad.

Now I know for sure I cannot live without You.

You are all I have, and You are all I need.

You're the only thing I have going on for me.

So, help me to understand Your grace, Your love,

And the power of forgiveness so I can worship You again.

Help me to fully know that You love me unconditionally.

Nothing I do can separate me from Your love.

Please, Father, help me!

Deliver me from all unrighteousness,

Set me free from this state of depression,

Set me free from loneliness,

Set me free from oppression,

Set me free from the darkness of this world.

All I want and desire

Is to do what's right in Your sight.

Please, Father, take me back into Your presence.

I can't do it on my own.

The flesh is weak.

I need Your very strength and power

To rise again and be in Your presence.

I need Your very Spirit

To help me get back on track.

I feel empty without You.

I feel lost and confused without Your guidance.

Please take hold of me this evening

And lead me into Your presence,

For I miss You very much.

Show Me

Yes, Lord, I want to know You more.

I want to see Your glory manifested in my life.

I want to see dead things come to life in my life again.

I want to see You move in my life more than ever before.

I want to see a shift in my situation.

I want to see Your ways in my life.

So, Lord, show me how to love like You.

Show me how to walk like You.

Show me how to forgive like You.

Show me how to have compassion like You.

Show me how to give like You.

For I want to know You more.

It's true, Lord.

Your glory is what I desire

To see manifested in my life.

Your glory is what I hunger for

To see Your name magnified and praised in my life.

So, Lord, show me Your way,

For I want to see my condition change.

Show me the way to go,

For I want to see You like never before.

Unnoticed, Rejected, and Overlooked

It's Just Not the Time

Just Five Minutes

Not Qualified

I Can Do All Things

It's Just Not the Time

Trust me, you're not alone.

I know what this like.

For years I was invisible in their sights.

For years I cried out loud,

And they still didn't notice me.

Many have failed to see what I can do,

And many have mistreated me.

I tried everything I could think of

Just to get their attention.

I used every gift and talent to impress them.

I tried the front row seats,

The middle aisle seats,

The two-piece suit,

But they still failed to notice me.

Rather, they ignored me.

All because I did not have a title.

I was not important.

I did not have a name.

I did not look like one of them.

I had neither fame nor status.

In their eyes I was nobody.

Trust me, I know what this like.

You're not alone.

I gave them my all, 100 percent.

For years, I waited to be noticed.

For years, I waited to be somebody in their eyes.

I waited and waited for one to at least notice me,

But no one did.

Let them overlook you.

Let them treat you as though you're nobody,

As though you have nothing to offer.

It's just not the season yet.

It's just not the time yet.

When the time is right,

Who will be able to overlook you?

You won't have to do anything to make them notice you.

Hang in there!

God knows what He's doing.

He still working, orchestrating things,

Pouring out more into you.

For at the proper time

He will make sure they notice you.

At the proper time

They will know your name.

So, hang in there!

It's just not the time yet!

Just Five Minutes

If you only knew who I was,

You would not have skipped me.

If you only knew what I made up,

You would not have overlooked me.

If you only knew my heart,

You would not have singled me out.

You sought a more 'qualified' woman,

One who was physically fit,

One with a name, status, fame, and reputation.

When I was right in front of you,

You looked at the outward appearance

But failed to give me a fair chance

To see who was really behind this petite frame.

You said to yourself,

"No, I can't use her.

She's not one of us.

She doesn't have what it takes.

She's too weak and powerless.

Her status says it all.

I want one with power,

One with influence,

One with the gift,

One who's physically fit,

One I am accustomed to."

Sometimes I wonder,

Are you truly connected to Him?

Do you truly understand how He operates?

Why are you letting the size fool you?

Why are you letting the height fool you?

Why are you letting the outward appearance fool you?

Why are you letting my status fool you?

It will take only five minutes

For you to discover who I am.

Why not give me a chance,

Why skip me,

Why overlook me,

When you can put your search to an end?

Come on, just give five minutes of your time

And you'll discover

Who resides on the inside of me.

Not Qualified

You said, "I don't have what it takes,

But I'm already among you."

You said, "Another candidate is more qualified,

But your description described me."

You said, "I'm not good enough,

But you always call me when you need me."

Why do you put such a limit on me,

When I'm already in there doing free labor?

Why do you put a limit on me

When the very language you need is my native one?

I may not have the five years' experience,

But I have His ability to do all things,

Just as I am currently doing free labor.

Don't forget where you started now.

Don't forget where you came from.

You did not just get up there on your own.

It was He who placed you in your position

When you had no experience.

It was He who cause you to find favor with men

When you had no set of skills.

Please do not say I don't have what it takes

When you were once me,

Fresh out of college

And always called me to come and assist those in need.

Don't be fooled by my lack of experience,

Thinking I don't have what it takes.

Haven't you heard that if He's done it for you,

He will do it for me too?

Who are you to say I'm not talented enough?

Who are you to say that I'm not qualified

When I have a helper that lives on the inside of me?

Are you sure you didn't make a mistake

By wanting to say 'overqualified' instead of 'not qualified'?

Because His Word says,

"I can do all things through Him who gives me strength."

(Philippians 4:13)

I Can Do All Things

I do not need your approval,

For I know who I am and whose I am.

I am indeed well equipped to do all things,

Designed and created by God

With an identity in Christ.

And a can-do attitude to accomplish all things

Not by might, nor by power, but by His Spirit.

Yes, I can in fact do all things.

Look around you:

Was there anything He called me to do

That I did not accomplish?

Who are you to tell me

What I can do and cannot do?

Who are you to tell me

I'm too weak and too small?

In case you did not know,

I belong to the King of kings,

The one who calls me 'friend,'

The Creator of heaven and earth,

The One who knows me inside-out.

Yes, I can do all things

For it is He who gives men the ability and power to gain
wealth.

It is He who gives men special talents, skills, and ability to
glorify Him.

So, yes, I can do all things.

(Zechariah 4:6; John 15:15; Deuteronomy 8:18; Exodus 31:3–5)

Suicidal Thoughts, Voices, and Negative Words

Hope in Him Is Life

Get behind Me

I Will Not Die

Still Standing

I Am Confident

Who Are You?

Hope in Him Is Life

I know you've been searching for some time now.

I know you've been longing for years and years.

I know you've been crying,

Pouring your heart and soul out to others.

You've searched and searched all around you,

You've traveled all over the continents

You can't find anybody who understands you—

Anybody to help and rescue you.

You spent every dime in therapy.

You wonder,

"Is there anyone out there who can relate to me?

Is there anyone out there who feels my pain?

Is there anyone out there who cares about me?"

I get you. I know exactly what you're saying.

Deep inside you is filled with the feeling

Of forsaken, abandonment, betrayal, scorn, rejection,

disappointment, hopelessness, loneliness, and emptiness.

At times you find yourself feeling guilty and sorry.

Then you say to yourself,

"Why should I live another day

In this careless, unloved, judgmental, and lonely world?

Why should I continue to torture myself?"

At night you forced yourself to sleep,

But with the hope you don't wake up the next day

Just so you could finally rest in peace.

You say to yourself,

"Who would care anyway

If I don't wake up the next day?

No one cares about my existence.

Truly, I have nothing to offer anyone.

So why live?

I am worthless.

There's nothing good in me.

There's nothing out there for me."

But guess what?

I think you got it all wrong.

You've had your eyes on the wrong things.

You've been listening to the wrong voices.

Your hope is in the wrong thing.

Your trust and confidence are in the wrong people.

Don't you know that hope in them will disappoint you?

Trust and confidence in them will also disappoint you?

Listening to the wrong voice will kill and destroy you?

You can't put your hope and trust in them.

You can't put your confidence in them.

You can't listen to them.

They will disappoint you in a split second.

But I'm here to tell you,

Don't give up yet.

I have good news for you:

I know One whose love is the everlasting love,

Who is faithful to all His promises,

A promise keeper,

A loving One,

A forgiving One,

A trustworthy One

A healer,

A Savior.

His name is Jesus,

Spells J-E-S-U-S,

One Who loves you unconditionally.

Nothing can separate you from His love.

In fact, He knew you

Before you were formed in your mother's womb.

He gave His life for you.

I don't know if you know this,

But you are not your own.

You belong to Him.

Trust me, He is who He says He is.

He will never disappoint you,

Nor forsake you,

Nor look down on you.

If you put your confidence in Him,

He will not disappoint you.

Hope without Him is death,

But hope in Him is life.

(Psalm 27:10, 145:13, 146:3; Romans 8:38–39; Jeremiah 1:5; Galatians 1:4)

Get Behind Me

That's right, I said it—

Get behind me.

I recognize your voice

And know all your tricks.

I know what you came to do:

You came to deceive me like Judas Iscariot,

Like you did to the neighbors not too long ago,

Reminded them of their past mistakes and failures,

Filled their hearts with guilts and shames,

Whispered in their ears, "It's too late.

It's over! There's no way out for you."

I know what you came to do:

You came to erase me from the face of the earth,

An earth that's not even yours,

An earth formed and established by my heavenly Father.

You came to kill, steal, and destroy me.

Sorry, you can't have me.

Sorry, you can't destroy me.

I now know who I am and whose I am.

My soul belongs to Him.

I was bought at a price.

Therefore, get behind me,

Father of Lies.

No, you will not have my soul.

What do you know about me?

Did you form me in my mother's womb?

Do you know the number of my hairs?

I know what you came to do.

I know what you're trying to do.

Sorry, you've got the wrong person today.

You will not have me.

Not today, tomorrow, or ever.

So, get behind me.

(Matthew 16:23, 27:5; John 10:10, 1 Corinthians 6:20; John 8:44; Luke 12:7; Psalm 118:17)

I Will Not Die

I refuse to listen to your lies.

You're a liar!

As a matter of fact, Father of Lies,

This isn't my final destination.

I will not leave this earth in this condition,

Nor will I stay in it any longer,

For all His promises to me are 'yes' and 'amen,'

And He is not a man who would lie

Nor a son of man who would change his mind.

Therefore, I rebuke you today.

Yes, He has a plan for my life.

Yes, in all things He works

For the good of those who love him

And have been called according to His purpose.

Liar! I will live my full potential.

I will experience all He has in store for me.

I will see these dead things come to life.

I will see all my dreams come to pass.

I will not die

But live and fulfill my destiny.

(John 8:44; 2 Corinthians 1:20; Numbers 23:19; Romans 8:28)

Still Standing

Thirty years later? No!

Who would have thought?

That wasn't the agenda he had for my life.

In fact, I never dreamt of that two-digit number.

I didn't think I could live to see it,

Nor did I know they had my name on it.

The plan was to destroy me for good,

Not to live to see this very day,

Writing to help save someone's life.

Had you told me thirty years later,

I would still be breathing,

I would not have believed you.

Truly, I should not be alive today.

I should have been gone twenty-seven years ago

When he told me I would never be anything in life

And wished I contracted a deadly disease.

I should have been gone twenty-five years ago
When he encouraged me to go ahead and stick the knife in.
I should have been gone twelve years ago
When he whispered in my ears and said,
"You are worthless.
You don't have anything to offer.
You're not beautiful.
Why don't you just die?
No one wants you."

In fact, about a year ago, he mumbled curses,
"What can you do? You cannot do anything."
Believe it or not,
I was supposed to be gone eight months ago
When I found myself in the middle of the expressway
Surrounded by cars and trucks.

As you see, he tried to erase me
From the face of the earth
As you would think he was my maker,

The one who had chosen me

Before He laid the foundation of this world.

But little did he know

The number of my days were already ordained

And multiplied by my Father.

He had already satisfied me with long life.

Yes, I should have been dead,

But I am still standing by God's grace.

(Ephesians 1:4; Genesis 6:7; Psalm 91:16)

I am Confident

Go ahead and say it.

I know what you're trying to say:

"Where is her God?"

Yes, it has lingered for some time.

Yes, I called upon His name, and He has yet answered me.

Yes, it's obvious that I am still in the same condition.

Yes, I felt forsaken and overlooked at times.

I know you're wondering, where is her God?

Doesn't He promise to never leave her or forsake her?

Moreover, He will supply all her needs.

But where is her God,

The One mighty to save and mighty to deliver?

Isn't nothing impossible with Him?

But I say to you: Quiet!

You and I know His Word will never return void.

Therefore, I am confident

That He is working behind the scenes,

Getting ready to blow your mind.

I am confident

That I will see my situation once more turn around.

So, go ahead and say it.

It will not be long

Before you will see His glory manifest in my life,

And when you yourself will bow down and worship Him.

(Psalm 27:13, Philippians 4:19, Isaiah 55:1

Who Are You?

Did you just say,

"Apart from you I am nothing?"

Is that what I just heard you say?

But my question for you is:

Who are you?

How long have I known you?

Where were you when God created life in me?

Come again?

"Apart from you I am nothing!"

But my question for you is,

Who are you?

Tell me, where does my ability and power to learn come

from?

Did you fill me with the Spirit of God,

Wisdom, understanding, knowledge,

And all kinds of skills?

Did I learn to read and reason through you?

Tell me, where does my intelligence come from?

And where do my gifts and talents come from?

You, Father of Lies,

Last time I read,

It is in Him I live, move, and have my being.

Last time I read,

It is He who gives man the ability and power to gain wealth.

And last time I read,

Apart from Him I can do nothing.

Every good and perfect gift is from above.

Again, who are you?

I know what you are after.

You want the praise that only belongs to Him.

You want the glory only He deserves.

Sorry, you can't have it.

And He won't share it with you.

He doesn't give His glory to another

Or His praise to idols.

(Exodus 35:35; Acts 17:28; James 1:17; John 15:5; Deuteronomy 8:18; Isaiah 42:8)

Stress and Anxiety

Get Back

It's Not Too Late

Be Still, Soul

He's Not Done Yet

Still on the Throne

He Has the Power

Indeed, He's Good

Not Once, Not Twice

Get Back

Tell me, what just got into me?

I must have woken up on another planet.

I must have been in a dream.

This isn't my nature,

Not even one of my weaknesses.

Me, anxious?

Me, afraid?

I must be in some kind of dream.

I must be under stress.

Could it be the delay that is causing me to be anxious?

I don't remember ever having to wait for this long.

I don't remember You taking this long to answer me.

You have always been on time.

To the contrary, You always show yourself faithful

And You're never an hour late.

I'm wondering what got into me suddenly.

Did You just leave the throne or something?

Because last time I checked, You were there.

Please tell me I'm just dreaming.

For anxiety has never been an issue for me.

Great faith is what I'm known for.

In fact, it was Your Spirit

Who determined which gift to give me.

Trust and believe are what I do best for the most part,

And it has been twenty years since I owned those names.

Through them you've done wonders in my life

And brought me to where I am today.

You have never failed to come to my rescue

Or make a way for me.

What has gotten into me

That I'm suddenly anxious about things?

Maybe I've lost track of what You've done in the past.

Maybe I've taken my eyes off of You.

I don't recall having to wait and see what happens next.

When You say go, I go.

When You say move, I move.

When You say wait, I'm still.

Now, suddenly, I can't move forward?

No, I must trust You and get back on track.

(Philippians 4:6; Proverbs 18:25; 1 Corinthians 12:11)

It's Not Too Late

Trust me when I say
It's not the end,
And it's not too late.
Trust me when I say
It isn't over yet,
So, be of good courage!
The Lord is mighty and strong in battles.

It doesn't matter
What it looks like.
It doesn't matter
Who is in the current position.
This is not the end.
A shift can still take place today.
You haven't been defeated.
God is still in control.

So today I encourage you
To be of good courage
And know that the earth is His
And everything in it,
The world and all who live in it.
It's not too late
For Him to turn it around.
It's not too late
For Him to bring change.

He can still remove men from their positions
And place you right where you belong.
He can still make a way out of no way.
Be of good courage!
It's not too late.
God can still bring it to pass.

(Psalm 24:1, 8)

Be Still, Soul

Holy Spirit,

Help this soul of mine be still

And know that my God

Is not a liar.

Spirit of truth,

Help this soul of mine be still
And know that my Heavenly Father
Will never fail me.
My Counselor,
Help this soul of mine be still
And know that my Heavenly Father
Is God.

I ask you to take control of my mind
And remind me of the plans my God has for me,
The plans to give me hope and a future.
Yes, Spirit of God,
Take control of my mind and rule over it.
Take away anything that troubles it on this day.
Wash and renew it.

I may not see a way out,
But that doesn't mean He doesn't have one.
I will say of the Lord
He is my way-maker, my deliverer,
My God in whom I put my trust and confidence.
Yes, soul, be still

And know that my Father is God

So, I say unto you this morning

To be still

And know that He has a plan for me.

(Psalm 46:10; Jeremiah 29:11)

He's Not Done Yet

Why are you panicking?

Why lose sleep worrying about tomorrow?

Haven't you heard

Tomorrow has enough trouble of its own?

Haven't you heard

Tomorrow doesn't promise us?

Did He tell you He was done with you?

Is He still in the grave?

Wasn't He raised on the third day?

Hasn't He rescued you before?

Didn't He make a way for you yesterday?

So why are you afraid?

Is there a situation He cannot turn around?

Is there a mountain He cannot move?

O you little doubter,

Where is your faith?

Last time I read

He was still the same miracle-working God.

You don't need to be anxious.

You don't need to worry.

God is working out the details of your life.

If you're not where you need to be,

He's not done yet.

(Hebrews 13:8; Matthew 6:25)

Still on the Throne

O soul, wake up!

Wake up and praise the great King!

Wake up and exalt Him!

You must wake up and bless Him,

For He has not changed.

He's still the same from yesterday,

Still seated on His holy throne.

Wake up and magnify His name,

For you and I know He is not a man who would lie

Nor a son of man who would change His mind.

When He speaks, He acts.

When He promises, He fulfills.

So, on this day, I command you to wake up

And worship the one and only King,

The One who has been good to you,

The One who has revealed Himself to you.

Wake up! Wake up! And worship Him!

You have no reason to feel down today.

You have no reason to be anxious about anything,

For He has been faithful to you.

He has been good to you.

He has never left your side.

So, wake up and praise Him for who He is,

For He is still on the throne.

(Numbers 23:19; Philippians 4:6)

He Has the Power

Tell me, why be anxious

When He is with all powers in His hands?

Why mourn day and night

When He hasn't spoken a word yet

Nor exercised His power?

Why lose hope

When you can just trust Him

With the plans He has for you?

Don't you get it?

He's the same from yesterday, today, and forever

The God of all ages,

The God from ancient days!

Why do you fret

When He reigns forever,

When He is the God of Glory,

The God of restoration,

And the God of justice?

As the angel asked Sarah,

"Is anything too hard for the Lord?"

He is not limited by these results.

What just happened was not by accident.

Trust me when I say it's not over—

At least believe me when I say,

He has the power

To turn it around for your good.

(Ephesians 3:21; Daniel 7:22; Psalm 37:7)

Indeed, He's Good!

I will testify, for I've tasted His goodness.

And yes, He is indeed good

And most worthy of praise.

I have seen His mighty acts,

And no one works like Him.

He not only fulfills my desires with good things

But with more than I expected.

He healed my broken heart

And filled it with joy and gladness.

Yes, the Lord is good indeed.

He gave me the ability

To accomplish everything set before me.

He always causes me to triumph in every trial.

He gives me victory over my enemies.

He shows up when I least expect it

Full of surprises,

Always on time,

Always making a way out of nowhere.

He opens doors no man can shut

And closes doors no man can open.

Indeed, He is good.

Not one of His promises fails

To come to pass in my life.

Yes, my soul will bless the Lord,

For He is good.

He turns bad reports to praise reports

And fights my every battle.

Bless the Lord, O my soul,

For the Lord is good indeed.

(Psalm 27:6–14, 34:8, 118:7, 145:19)

Not Once, Not Twice

I sought the Lord.

Yes, I sought the Lord with all my heart,

And He revealed Himself to me,

Not once, not twice,

But too many times to count.

He redeemed me from all the cares of this world

And rescued me from a deep hole.

He calms my anxious heart,

And now it is still.

Truly the Lord can be found

If you seek Him with all your heart,

For my anxiety is no more,

My fears are gone,

My confusions are no more,

Situations turned around,

Chains loosened and broken.

I sought the Lord with all my heart,
And I found Him.
He revealed Himself to me,
Not once, not twice,
But too many times to count.
He redeemed my life from sin and death.
He set me free from captivities, bondages,
And generational curses.
He saved me from the darkness of this world,
From anything not like Him,
And now I am free.

Yes, I sought the Lord,
And He revealed Himself to me,
Not once, not twice,
But too many times to count.
Go ahead and seek Him
While He may be found,
For I sought the Lord,
And He revealed Himself to me.

He set me free

From all the cares of this world,

Not once, not twice,

But too many times to count.

Doors once closed are now opened.

Conditions unchanged are now changed.

Bad reports are now praise reports.

Nos are now yeses.

Setbacks are now setups and set-forths.

I sought the Lord.

He restored my life.

He took me from faith to faith.

Yes, the Lord is near to those

Who seek Him with all their hearts.

For I sought the Lord.

And He delivered me

Not once, not twice,

But too many times to count.

(Psalm 34:4; Jeremiah 29:13; Isaiah 55:6)

Identity Crisis and Confusion

Who Do You Say I Am?

The Living God

You May Not Understand

Just the Way I Am

He's Mighty

Who Do You Say I Am?

Some say they know me

But have no idea who I am.

They defined me by my past,

My present condition, and my status

But have no idea who He says I am.

They let other people's opinion of me define me

But failed to ask my Master about me,

The One who created life in me.

When they see me,

They see two decades ago,

Yesterday, ordinary, teen mom,

Homeless, burden, poor,

Unstable, unemployed, needy,

And always struggling.

They say among themselves, "I know her.
I remember her very well."

Then I asked, "Lord, are these true?
Tell me: Who do you say I am?"
He then whispered and said,
"You are a masterpiece,
Chosen before I laid the foundation of this world."

"You were bought at a price,
My chosen one,
A royal priesthood,
My special possession.
That's who you were,
That's what you are,
And that's who you will always be."

"When I look at you,
I see set apart, chosen one,
My glory, purpose, and destiny.
You're not your own,

Nor do you belong to them.

You are mine."

"In fact, I called you 'friend'

And tell you great, unsearchable things

You did not know.

You are my child,

That's who you are!"

(Matthew 16:13–20; Jeremiah 33:3)

The Living God

What a privilege to know God.

Not the man-made one—the blind, mute,

And dead statue who can only stay put

That neither knows my name nor cares about me.

I mean the living God,

The Creator of heaven and earth,

The One who actually speaks, sees, hears, moves, and acts,

The One who formed me in my mother's womb.

In fact, in Him I live, move, and have my being.

The glorious God,

The One who lives and reigns forever,

The God of Abraham, Isaac, and Jacob

Whose faithfulness endures forever.

He's the great 'I Am.'

My God knows my name

And always answers me when I call on Him.

Not only that, He can see my tears

And give ever-present help when I am in trouble.

He is mighty to save and deliver.

What an honor to know the God of Abraham, Isaac, and Jacob,

The Living God, the great 'I Am,'

The God of gods and Lord of lords,

One who is near to those who call on Him,

To those who call on Him in truth.

My God can move, act, and save.

Indeed, when He speaks, He acts,

And when He promises, He fulfills.

O, how blessed I am to know the living God,

The great and magnificent God who reigns forever!

(Acts 17:28; Matthew 22:32; Psalm 46:1; Deuteronomy 10:17; Hebrews 13:8)

You May Not Understand

Some said I'm amazing, smart, beautiful, and a Christian.

One said, by far he had not met anyone like me.

"You are beautiful!" one texted me once.

"I've never met anyone who speaks like you.

You are such an excellent messenger for our Lord.

Are you ready to date?

What's your feeling? Your situation?"

Shockingly, one is losing his patience with me

Just one week after we've been texting each other.

"Sorry, working on my patience," he said.

"Just can't wait to meet you.

Let me know when you'd like to meet again."

"Yes, I'm ready to date!" I exclaimed.

Some shouted, "It's a date! See you soon."

And some can't wait to chat on the phone

While some hide behind their text messages,

Feeling flattered that someone is excited to meet me.

O, how I enjoyed getting to know them over the phone!

How I enjoyed talking to them!

I can't wait to finally meet them!

Thrilled that this one is a man of God,

Thrilled that some are God-conscious men,

Could this one finally be the one? I thought.

Before I could step my foot to my doorstep,

The notification buzzer went off:

A message from one after our third date.

"Hi, thanks for meeting up after your day.

You looked great. I had a fun time.

Thanks for the good company. Nice to see you."

"Hi, you're welcome to come up to my place to watch a movie."

"Sounds good. How about you learn a little bit more about me?"

"Hello, are we still on for today?"

Waiting and hoping to hear a word,

Surprisingly, no follow-up call or text message.

Days went by, no text.

Weeks went by, no calls.

Months went by, no emails.

Then I wonder, What's wrong with me?

Why can't I keep a man?

Why are they leaving me suddenly?

Why they are disappearing so quickly?

Why they are rejecting me?

Am I cursed?

Then I heard a voice say, "No, my daughter,

Nothing is wrong with you.

Everything I made is good.

You are fearfully and wonderfully made.

You may not understand it,

But trust me, I know what I'm doing.

I know good gifts to give to my children.

They didn't just get up and leave,

They didn't just disappear,

It is I who removed them out of your life.

They were unstable and wasting your time

I had to removed them out of your life

To make room for the one I have designed for you.

My daughter, you're not cursed!

I'm just watching out for you.

Take heart!

The one I have for you

Will understand your worth and will stay."

Just the Way I Am

Wow, I can't believe He loves me just the way I am!

I mean, I don't need to pretend to be something I'm not.

I don't need to look a certain way for Him to love me.

I don't have to be any taller or shorter for Him to love me.

He loves me just the way I am!

Gaining or losing weight, He still loves me.

Uptight or reserved, He still loves me.

Employed or unemployed, He still loves me.

He loves me just the way I am.

I don't need to get a nose job for Him to love me.

I don't have to get a breast implant for Him to love me.

I don't need any facelift or wrinkle-remover for Him to love me.

He loves me just the way I am.

With or without a bank account, He still loves me.

Feeling down or weak, He still loves me.

College degree or not, He still loves me.

Low self-esteem or lack of self-confidence, He still loves me.

He loves me just the way I am.

Truly, I don't need to have status, fame, wealth,

Or good reputation for Him to love me.

Don't you get it? He loves me just the way I am.

For my Maker is my husband,

The Lord Almighty is His name!

Yes, I'll say it again:

He loves me just the way I am.

(Isaiah 54:5)

He Is Mighty!

Have you found anybody like Him yet?

One who is all wise and all knowing?

One whose ears are attentive to our cries?

One who saves those crushed in spirit?

Have you found anybody like Him yet

Who can tell you great, unsearchable things you do not know?

Who offers ever-present help in times of trouble?

See, you don't understand.

You don't get it.

There isn't one out there like Him

Nor will there ever be.

Don't let their words confuse you;

He alone is mighty!

When will you realize He is your last result,

And there is none out there like Him?

Trust me when I say, there isn't one out there.

I once walked in your shoes.
In fact, I searched and couldn't find anybody
Who was strong and mighty in battle.
I searched and couldn't find one
Who could make me walk in freedom.

Can't you see He is mighty to save you,
Mighty to deliver you,
And His name is mighty in power?
Trust me when I say He is mighty,
For I know what it's like to be delivered and set free.
He is my deliverer, my provider, my protector, my healer,
My strong tower and defense.
I can testify: Yes, He is mighty!
And His name is mighty in power!

(Psalm 34:15, 18, 46:1; Jeremiah 33:3; Jeremiah 10:6)

Unloved and Worthless

A Hidden Treasure

No Other Choice

You're All I Need

Your Love Is Enough for Me

A Hidden Treasure

Don't walk away yet!

There's no other one out there.

You may not find another one,

For it is rare to find—

A one of a kind,

Hidden treasure.

Who can find it?

If you're looking for yellow, you won't find it.

If you're looking for white, you won't find it.

If you're looking for rose, you won't find it.

For it is colorless with its own shape.

Truly it doesn't carry the wealth, riches, power, and status

One is accustomed to.

Rather, it is rich in faith, love, joy, peace,

Understanding, and compassion—
A pure and passionate heart.
Who can find it out there?
A heart of gold.
Who can you compare it to?

There's none like it out there.
It's not a man-made one,
But a hidden treasure created
And shaped by the Almighty God.

No Other Choice

What choice do I have?

Don't good gifts come from You?

I've tried it all, but nothing seems to work.

Only You can understand my worth

And bless me with the desire of my heart,

For no one seems to understand my true worth in You.

Therefore, I have no choice

But to surrender them to you.

See, I have searched all over,

But I couldn't find anyone

To keep their promises to me.

Only You, Lord, are faithful to Your promises,

And all Your promises are yes and amen.

Many have disappointed me

And failed to see the woman I am in you,

The one of a kind you have created,

The God-fearing and devoted woman,

The loveable, caring, and compassionate woman I am in you.

I've done all I can, but nothing seems to work.

I've used them all just to impress them.

As you see, I have no more gifts left to use.

Who besides You

Knows good gifts to give to their children?

Who besides You

Knows the plans You have for me?

Therefore, I have no other choice but to give it all to You—

The desires, the dreams, the wants.

(James 1:17; Matthew 5:37; 2 Corinthians 1:20; James 1:17; Jeremiah 29:11)

You're All I Need

Why waste my energy

Trying to find somebody

To look at me and validate me

When I already know that I am loved

By a King unconditionally?

Why waste my time

Trying to find somebody

To understand my worth

When He alone understands and knows

That I am His masterpiece and one of a kind?

Tell me, why try so hard and hope

That they see something in me

When He knows me inside-out?

You'd better wake up, self,

And understand your true worth in Him.

You were bought at a price,

A child of destiny,

God's special instrument,

A chosen one,

A very talented one

With many gifts and abilities.

You don't need somebody

Who can't seem to understand your worth in Him.

You don't need somebody

Who fails to see what's on the inside of you.

You don't need somebody

Who thinks you are too holy for them,

When God Himself is Holy.

You don't need somebody

Who doesn't know what they want.

God, you are all I want and all I need.

You, who love and accept me just the way I am.

No unstable and unsure ones,

But you, O Lord.

Your Love Is Enough for Me

Today, for the first time,

I can honestly say that I am content with You.

Who would have thought that today

The desire to be loved by one of your sons

Is not as strong as it was four years ago?

Who would have thought that this dream

Would someday fade away?

A dream that pounded in my heart nonstop for decades

And refused to die is finally fading away.

As a result of spending much time with You

And in Your presence, singing and praising You,

Hearing You whisper softly in my ears

That You love me unconditionally,

And reading about Your unconditional love for me,
I now realize that Your love
Is what I have waited for all my life.

Therefore, I must say now that I am content with You.
I am no longer feeling unloved, unwanted, and worthless,
For I am convinced that Your love is enough for me,
And it is far greater than any human love.

Fear, Doubts, Worry

O You of Little Faith

It's Not Too Hard

Don't Worry

Trust

I Serve a God

O You of Little Faith

Have you not heard

The Lord is the same

From yesterday, today, and forever?

Have you not seen

The marvelous things

He has done for me recently?

You asked, "Do you have a job there?"

But my question for you is:

Who formed the earth and established it?

Isn't He the Lord?

Why are you worrying

About my tomorrows?

Why are you worrying

About my future

When my future is in His hands,

Including the world?

Have you not heard

The Lord owns the earth and everything in it?

The world and all who live in it?

So why are you worrying

About my next provision

When He is my provider?

O you of little faith,

Did His nature change?

Did Jesus leave His right side

And His Spirit is no more?

Why are you doubting His ability

To make a way for me over the other side

When He just made a way for me

Right before your very own eyes?

Have you not heard

The Lord is the everlasting God,

And He will supply all my needs?

O you of little faith,

Have I ever called upon Him

When He did not come to my rescue?

Why are you wasting your time and energy

Worrying about my life over the other side

When you can just pray and watch Him do it again?

O you of little faith,

Is anything too hard for the Lord?

Is there a situation He cannot turn around?

Is there a condition He cannot change?

Besides, who directs my steps?

Who else determine the place and time where I should live?

Why are you worrying

About my tomorrows

When you can't even add

An hour to them?

Why are you worrying

About my life

When you don't even know

The number of my days?

O you of little faith,

Don't you know

If He did it before,

He'll do it again?

(Matthew 8:26; Hebrews 13:8; Psalm 24:1–2; Matthew 6:25;
Isaiah 40:28; Philippians 4:19; Genesis 18:14; Acts 17:26)

It's Not Too Hard

It's not a question whether He is able.

It's not a question of how big it is.

It's not a question of how long it has been.

Who do you know?

Your status?

Your position in life?

Don't you get it?

Nothing is too hard for Him!

Indeed, He is the

God of all ages,

The God of miracles,

The God of wonders,

The same miracle-working God

From ancient days.

It's not a question

Whether He can save you or deliver you.

It's not a question

Whether He can set you free or not.

It's not a question

Whether He still performs miracles.

Truly, it's about,

Do you believe in the impossible?

Do you perceive it?

Do you have enough faith to receive it?

Can you see it manifesting in the physical realms?

For nothing is impossible with Him,

So, it's not that it's too hard,

It's just can you get rid of your doubts

To see it come to pass?

(Luke 1:37)

Don't Worry

I bet you don't know my name or my background

Because if you did,

You would not stop talking to me.

Clearly you do not know my history

Because if you did,

You would not keep looking me up and down.

Why stop talking to me

When you don't even know anything about me

Or even try to know me?

Why stop interacting with me

When you still have your position?

You used to say hi,

But you stopped suddenly.

It's okay—you can still smile when you see me.

You can still greet me.

You don't have to stop.

My position is just temporary.

If you only knew what my purpose here on earth is,

You would not stop talking to me.

Please don't let this chair I'm sitting on fool you

Or the glass door fool you.

I know that sitting behind the glass

Can appear as though I have arrived.

But allow me to tell you

A little bit about me.

I know you don't know this,

But I have a greater purpose in life.

This isn't my destination.

This isn't my passion

Or my calling in life.

Rest assured—

I'm just passing by.

I am not here looking for a title,

Nor am I here to rule over you.

In fact, they offered me multiple,

And I declined them all.

Don't worry! I do not want your job.

I want one that is meaningful,

One through which I can touch lives

And make a difference.

In fact, my purpose is greater than your very position,

One that is bigger than me.

You don't have to worry—

I'm just here working for a greater purpose,

That is, saving money to fulfill my destiny.

Trust

It was never my intention

To not fully trust You with all my heart

When You have proven Yourself to me

Day after day.

It was never my intention

To rely on my own understanding

When Your ways are better than mine

And Your thoughts are higher than mine.

I didn't mean to doubt

Your plans for my life and their timing.

I may not be where I want to be,

But I am not where I used to be

Twenty years ago.

Truly You have done wonders in the past

And had revealed Yourself to me,

Even in my dead situations.

You've showed Yourself faithful to me

And have not forsaken me.

But please understand that being in my condition

For year after year is not easy.

Sorry if I am leaning on my own understanding

And jumping to conclusions.

You alone know the plans You have for me.

It's just that this season

Seems a little longer than any other season.

You've never taken this long

To reveal Yourself to me

And get me over to the next season.

I'm sure You can understand.

I no longer want to lean on my own understanding.

I want to trust You with the process,

Including the delays and setbacks.

I want to acknowledge You more in all my ways

So that You can make my path straight to my destiny.

Lord, help me to fully trust You with the process

And not lean on my own understanding.

(Proverbs 3:5–6; Isaiah 55:8–9)

I Serve a God

You may doubt the very things

I am about to say to you.

You may not understand the very words

That will come out of my mouth.

But I do know Him

And can testify about Him.

Trust me when I say

I know the God I serve—

Not a dead one

But the living One,

Not a man-made one

But the Creator of all mankind,

One who is most worthy of praise

And whose faithfulness continues

From generation to generation.

You may not believe me.

You may think I am out of my mind

Or on some kind of medication.

However, last time I checked,

I was in my right mind.

In fact, I have the mind of Christ.

Believe me, I know what I am talking about.

For I have seen His very power at work in my life.

Truly, I know the God I serve.

Indeed, I serve a God

Who is faithful to all His promises,

And all His promises are yes and amen.

I serve a God

Who goes before me

In battles day and night.

And who is strong and mighty in battles.

I serve a God—

If He is on my side, I can't lose.

And if He is for me,

No one can be against me.

You may doubt the very word

I'm about to share with you.

You may not understand me,

But trust me when I say

I know the God I serve.

For I serve a God

Who is the God of completion.

When He starts, He finishes.

I serve a God who specializes

In fresh and new revelation every day

And who's always revealing Himself to me.

Truly I serve a God

Who watches over my coming and going

So that no weapons formed against me shall prosper.

O, I serve a God

Who knows my end from the beginning,

Who is not intimidated by any of life storms—

The God who knows my very destiny.

You may not believe the very words I just shared with you.

But I serve a God who is able to reveal Himself to you

And deliver you right where you are.

You don't need to fear,

For the God I serve is big enough to rescue you.

(Psalm 119:90, 121:8, 145:3, 13; 2 Corinthians 1:20; Philippians 1:6; Isaiah 54:17)

Love and Intimacy

My First True Love

Dancing with My Father

There's None

You Are Beautiful

He's Faithful

The One and Only

I Love You, Lord

My First True Love

He might have been the first,

But just realizing now

That I was wrong the entire time,

Claiming someone else for over a decade

Who is no longer around,

When You are right here next to me.

Just realizing now how I missed the entire truth,

Acknowledging someone else

Who is nowhere to be found today.

How did I let that happen?

How did I miss that

When you are the One who so loved me

And gave Your one and only Son for me,

When He is the One who laid down His life for me?

Just realizing now how I mistook someone else for You

When You are the One

Who taught me the true meaning of love,

When You are the One

Who first loved me

And made Yourself known to me,

I'm wondering how I failed to realize that

When You were the One

Who sacrificed Your life for me

And paid the penalty for my sins,

How did I miss that

When You are the One who died for me

That I may live?

Truly, I didn't know what love was

Until I saw You that day.

I didn't know the meaning of love

Until I saw a picture of the cross.

I didn't know what love was

Until I learned how You laid Yourself down for me.

I wonder how I failed to acknowledge You first.

How did I miss that

When you gave up Your life for me?

Indeed, You are my first true love,

A love nothing can separate me from,

A love that is unconditional

And will never leave me,

An everlasting love,

A love that is dear to my heart.

He might have been the first,

But just realizing now

That You are my heart

And my first true love,

I love You, Lord!

(John 3:16; 1 John 3:16; Romans 3:24–25; 2 Corinthians 5:15; Romans 8:38–39)

Dancing with My Father

O how blessed I was to have that dance with You today, Dad!

How blessed I was actually dancing with You,

The One who created life in me,

The One who knows me inside out.

Indeed, You are a good partner to have.

I loved and enjoyed Your presence.

I liked the way You pulled me close to You and did not let me go.

Truly, I was impressed by how You took hold of my right hand.

I didn't know You have all these other great moves in you,

Besides Your moving things in my life from time to time.

I know You said, "It's in you I live, move, and have my being,"

But I was blown away by Your anointing,

Moving me one place to another.

For once I couldn't stand still to dance.

For once I had to let go of someone's hands.

I had no choice but to let them go

And bow down and worship You—

All because Your presence overtook me.

When can we dance again?

It was in Your presence I felt most free, safe, and secured.

After the dance, I didn't have to worry that You were going

to leave.

I didn't have to worry of what was going to happen next.

I trusted You.

I hope this was not our last dance,

For I want to dance with You more.

I want to experience more of Your presence.

Please tell me we'll have a chance to dance again,

For I only desire to dance with my Father.

(Psalm 139:13; Acts 17:28; Isaiah 41:13)

There's None

It has been twenty years since I've been waiting

To find One who is perfect in all His ways,

One who will love me unconditionally,

One who will never leave me nor forsake me,

One who will understand my worth,

And One who will go before me and fight for me.

Yes, Lord, it has been some time now

Since I've been waiting to see

If there's anyone out there like You,

But I can't seem to find One who is strong and mighty,

One who never loses any battles,

And One who is an ever-present help

In times of trouble.

Truly there's none like You, O God.

There's no one I can find

Who is faithful to all His promises.

You are absolutely right!

Indeed, there is none like You.

No one can love me like You do.

No one can fight my battles like You do.

You alone are God and faithful to all Your promises.

There's none, and never will there be one,

Like you, O God.

(Hebrews 13:5; Psalm 24:8; 46:1)

You Are Beautiful

There's no doubt about it—

You are indeed beautiful, Lord.

Your beauty is magnificent.

O Lord, how beautiful and glorious You are!

No kings, no gods, no one out there

Share Your heavenly beauty.

I wonder where Your beauty

Can be displayed for the world to see

That You are the most beautiful King alive!

I wonder where Your beauty

Can be displayed for the universe to see

That You are the most beautiful Savior alive!

I wonder where Your beauty

Can be displayed for every continent to see

That You are the most beautiful Lord alive?

Where can Your beauty be displayed?

I think a cover of magazine is too small,
A billboard is too small,
A TV screen is too small to display that
You are the most beautiful Lord alive!

O Lord, You are beautiful.
You are not only beautiful—You are glorious.
You are not only glorious—You are magnificent.
You are not only magnificent—You are marvelous.
You are not only marvelous—You are excellent in all Your
ways.
I adore You, my beautiful King.

He's Faithful

Tell me, is there anybody like Him?

Is there someone out there who, when they speak, they act?

And when they promise, they fulfill?

I don't know about you,

But I have not found anybody like Him

Who is gracious and merciful.

I don't know about you, but I searched

And did not find anybody who is trustworthy.

I don't know about you,

But I have not found anybody who can supply all my needs.

Tell me, is there anybody like Him

Where by their stripes you are healed?

Is there anybody like Him

Where you call upon their name and you are saved?

I searched, but I could not find.

I knocked at the doors, but they couldn't open.

I asked, but they couldn't give.

Indeed, no one is like Him.

Is there anybody like Him

Who can fulfill the desire of your heart?

Who can you find out there

Who will let their yes be yes and their no be no?

Yes, He's faithful,

Faithful to His promises.

(Numbers 23:19; Hebrews 13:8; Philippians 4:19; Isaiah 53:5; Romans 10:13)

The One and Only

There's no other.

It is You I love with all my mind,

With all my soul,

And with all my strength.

It's always been You,

The one and only lover of my soul,

The One I love and adore.

Who can love me like You?

Who can replace You,

My very source of strength and joy?

It is You I adore,

It's always been You

And will forever be You.

Who can love me like You,

My Lord the King?

Who can forgive my sins

And remember them no more?

My breath of life, my maker, my husband, my salvation,

Who can restore health to me

And set me free from sickness, disease, and infirmities?

It's You I adore.

It's You I long to hear each and every morning.

It's You I desire to worship and magnify Your name,

For no one else knows my true worth,

No one else has died for me to live,

No one else has turned my sorrow to joy

But You alone,

So, You're the one and only one

Whom I can't live without,

For, apart from You, I can do nothing,

(Isaiah 43:25; Psalm 30:11; John 15:5)

I Love You, Lord

I love You, lover of my soul—

My very breath of life.

When can I go and be where You are?

I want to be right where You are,

For my soul longs for You.

I can't seem to get enough of Your presence;

The time I spent in Your presence is not enough.

All I desire is to be in Your presence more.

If I could, I would praise You around the clock 24/7,

But with a destiny to fulfill,

It's not possible.

O beautiful and magnificent Savior,

You who is perfect in all Your ways,

You who shows Yourself faithful to the faithful ones,

You who do not hold my past sins against me,

You, Your love for me is unconditional.

When can I be where You are to whisper in Your ear

And tell You that I love You?

I love You, Lord.

I love You with all my heart and with all my strength.

I love You more and more each day.

(Psalm 18:25, 30; Isaiah 43:25)

Victory and Justice

Victory Is Mine

In His Name

Too Small

No Choice

Dance Again

She's Free, Indeed

Best Defense Team

Who Can Be Against Me?

Victory Is Mine

So, you thought it was over,

And you got away with injustice, huh?

Did you really think I was alone that morning?

Did you really think I was one of your fraud victims

And didn't have one who stood behind me?

See, you don't understand,

You got it all twisted.

I was never alone when you saw me that morning.

Though you could not see Him,

He was with me the whole entire time.

In fact, when I inquired about it,

He was with me,

Guiding me throughout the process.

Before I headed your way,

He had already gone before me.

I was never alone.

He was present before the transaction,

During the transaction,

And after the transaction.

I was never alone.

Meeting you was a setup.

He saw all the injustice that was done to His children.

So, He used my weaknesses, my lack of knowledge,

To put a stop to your plans.

You didn't get away with injustice that morning.

You didn't win.

I was never a victim.

He let you have your way,

For He knew your time was coming.

Sorry if you got it all twisted.

You just happened to mess with the wrong person,

A child of God.

It was never over until He said it was over.

Sorry for the confusion.

Victory is always mine.

With Him on my side,

I can't lose.

In His Name

You said what?

No, trust me, we're not on the same page here.

I think you got the name mixed up.

I think you got it all twisted.

Are you sure we're talking about the same name, Jesus?

Jesus who was crucified, died, and rose on the third day?

In His name

Demons flee,

Knees bow,

Situations turn around,

Lives change and transform.

Clearly, we're not on the same page of the Holy Bible.

Who can stand against Him?

In His name

I cannot be defeated,

I cannot be stuck,

Not in His book,

Nor on earth,

Nor in heaven.

I think you got it all twisted,

For power is what I've known to be in His name.

Victory is what I've known to be in His name.

Deliverance is what I've known to be in His name.

Healing is what I've known to be in His name.

Breakthrough is what I've known to be in His name.

Restoration is what I've known to be in His name.

Peace and joy are what I've known be in His name.

I think you got it all twisted,

For in His name

I am victorious,

I am above and not beneath,

I am an overcomer,

I am more than a conqueror.

(1 Corinthians 15:4; Deuteronomy 28:13; Romans 8:37)

Too Small

I'm not sure if you believe in His existence.

Maybe you do but just deny His power.

I'm not sure if you've heard of Him before

Or even know His name.

But in case you don't know or forget about His nature,

Please allow me to tell you a little bit about Him.

Allow me to remind you of who He is,

So next time you don't waste your time and energy.

His name is, 'I AM,'

The God who created heaven and earth.

The earth is His and everything in it,

Including all powers.

He is the ancient God.

He is the God of truth, the God of justice,

And the One who has the final word.

I'm not sure if you know this,

But He decides who comes and goes.

He is in complete control.

No one gets in their positions on their own.

I know you are fighting hard to stop anyone who isn't like you.

I know you tried everything in your power to destroy them.

I know you are disruptive.

You are trying everything to stop them from reaching their

highest levels,

But you failed to recognize who sits in His holy throne.

Truly, you're too small to stop them.

You're too small to stop the process.

Who can reverse when He acts?

Haven't you learned from the past?

You have tried to stop her, too,

But you were not able to do so.

Now what makes you think this time you can stop this

One,

When He is the same God from yesterday and today and

forever,

When He is the One who is in complete control of this world?

With what power can you come up against this One?

For once, use your common sense and wake up.

You are too small to stop His plan!

(Exodus 3:13–15; Genesis 1:1; Isaiah 43:13; Hebrews 13:8)

No Choice

Dead situation, have you heard of the dry bones in the valley?

Dead condition, have you heard of the dry bones in the valley?

Dead season, have you heard of the dry bones in the valley?

At His order they all came back to life.

At His command every dead situation is turned around.

So, dead situation, dead condition, dead season,

Hear me out: you have no choice but to rise.

In the might of Jesus, I speak life to you today.

I speak blessings over you.

I speak harvest over you.

You have no choice

But to come to life.

You have no choice

But to change and turn around.

Hear me out: I will not die in this condition.

I wasn't born to live in poverty.

I wasn't born to live in mediocrity.

I wasn't born to live in lack.

God did not create me to be a borrower.

Therefore, in Jesus' name I speak life to you.

That's right! You have no choice

But to rise on this very day,

Not by might or power,

But by His Spirit, Rise!

(Ezekiel 37:1–14; Zechariah 4:6)

Dance Again

Hallelujah! It will not be long

Before God will part my Red Sea for me

And make a way in the wilderness for me,

When suddenly my phone will ring

And doors will begin to open,

When new opportunity will come my way left and right,

For the Lord has heard my prayers

And has taken them into consideration.

I will soon dance again—

Not just any dance, but a dance of victory over my enemies.

Hallelujah! It will not be long

Before the world will know my name

Including my Father's name, I AM WHO I AM, God.

For the Lord God has fought my battles and won my

victories.

He is getting ready to shame the wise and the strong.

My Father is getting ready to put me on display

And show me off to the world.

I will soon dance again—

Hallelujah, Hallelujah,

I will soon dance again before the Lord.

For the Lord God has won the victory.

(Exodus 3:14; Isaiah 43:19; 1 Corinthians 1:27)

She's Free, Indeed

If you had told her sixteen years ago

That one day that she would be a slave

To the darkness of this world,

She would not have believed you.

If you had told her a day is coming

Where she would give in to the flesh,

She would not have believed you.

Surprisingly, she wakes up one day

And finds herself in a world she isn't familiar with,

Inside a deep hole in which she has no business,

A place from which she had tried to set herself free,

But she could not.

Who would have thought, from time to time

She would revisit the place and find herself stuck?

Who would have thought she would find herself

Multiple times in that hole?

She never thought it could ever happen to her.

She did not know her emotion could be as powerful,

To where it controls her every move,

But she cried out to God for mercy,

And the Lord heard her and delivered her.

She once was stuck,

But He made a way for her to escape

With just a song of praise.

She was once a slave to sin,

But she has been set free,

For He whom the Son has set free

Is free, indeed.

Yes, today,

She's free, indeed!

(1 Corinthians 10:13; John 8:36)

Best Defense Team

So, tell me, who is this best defense team you've been
talking about?
The one I've heard of who never loses any case,
The one I've heard of who is strong and mighty in battles,
The one I've heard of who can plead your case
And shut the mouth of any accusers?

Yes, they are all wise and all-knowing.
They have never lost any cases—
Great reputation, great protector, great vindicator,
Always on your side and always for you.

You have heard correctly:
They are mighty to win and mighty to set you free.
No team is like this team, you know.
It won't be over until they say it's over!

When man says no, they say yes!

Nothing takes place without their permission.

They are three in one,

The Father, the Son, and the Holy Spirit.

Their angels will go before you

And prepare the way for you.

You don't need a number to call them.

Just call upon the name of the Lord,

And they will be there.

I tell you, they are

The best defense team on the earth.

(Romans 10:13; Luke 1:35)

Who Can Be Against Me?

Tell me, who can be against me

When all wealth, power, and possessions belong to Him?

Who can be against me

When He speaks, He acts,

And when He promises, He fulfills?

Who can actually stop me

From getting to where He wants me to be?

Who can oppose me

From having what I need in life

When He already promised to supply to all my needs?

I don't think you get it.

I don't think you understand.

Have you not heard

That the world and everything in it belongs to Him,

Including you and your financial institution?

Have you not heard
That He is the God of glory,
The God of miracles,
And the God of wonders?
Have you not heard
That He chose me
Before He laid the foundation of the earth?
I am His special instrument,
And He set me apart for His glory.

Truly, if God is for me, who can be against me?
If God says it's my time, who can delay me?
Please hear me out.
You do not have the last word over my life—
Nor demons, bad credit, or negative accounts from the past,
Nor can you stand against me.
You have no other choice but to approve me
In Jesus' name!

(Romans 8:31; Numbers 23:19; Psalm 24:1; Philippians 4:19)

Thankfulness

I Made Up My Mind

You Did It Anyway

My Daily Bread

Another Day

Through It All

I Made Up My Mind

Surely, I made up my mind

To rejoice and be glad on this day,

This very special day my heavenly Father has made

Where I am well and alive,

This very blessed day my Father has made

Where many have missed it,

This day where some have fallen into a deep sleep

And yet not sure if they will ever wake up again,

This very blessed day my heavenly Father has made

Where some are in chains and bondage,

Waiting to be set free

To proclaim His holy name

And the marvelous things He has done.

Yes, I made up my mind

To rejoice and be glad on this day,

This day where I have food on my table

And many will go hungry throughout the day,

This blessed day where many have lost their minds,

And yet I woke up with the mind of Christ,

This very special day I woke up with a roof over my head

And many are still out there in the cold, waiting for shelters,

This very blessed day where the sick await recovery,

And yet I am healed by His stripes.

Indeed, I made up my mind

To rejoice on this day

And enter into His gates with thanksgiving

And into His courts with praise

And approach His throne with boldness and confidence,

Giving Him thanks for all He has done for me.

Surely, I made up my mind to be glad on this day

And bless His name that is above all names

For His goodness in my life.

Yes, I will rejoice.

I will rejoice and glorify His name.

Yes, I will be glad in it.

I will be glad in it and magnify His holy name,

For this is the day the Lord has made

And called me to rejoice and be glad in it.

I will exalt Him,

For He has indeed blessed me.

I will glorify His name,

For He has revealed Himself to me,

He has supplied all my needs.

I will exalt Him,

For He has shown Himself strong to me.

This is the day the Lord has made.

I made up my mind

To rejoice and be glad in it.

(Psalm 100:4, 118:24; Isaiah 53:5; Philippians 2:9)

You Did It Anyway

Truly, Lord, you didn't have to breathe life into me this morning.

You didn't have to renew my strength and mind on this day.

You didn't have to refresh my anointing when I asked you for more.

You didn't have to strengthen me again,

But you did it anyway.

So, Lord, I thank you that you're not yet done with me.

Thank you that I am in my right mind this morning.

Thank you for your fresh anointing to accomplish all things.

Thank you for my ability to praise and bless you

In my present condition.

Yes, Lord, it's true!

You didn't have to be near me when I called on You today.

You didn't have to keep me in perfect peace when I asked
You to.

You didn't have to overshadow me with Your hands.

You didn't have to go before me to prepare the way for me
today.

But You did it anyway.

So, thank you, Lord, for Your faithfulness to all Your
promises.

Thank you, Lord, for Your peace that passes all understanding.

Thank you for Your divine protection over my life and
loved ones.

Thank you for being my defense, vindicator, and strong tower.

Again, You didn't have to release me in the power of the
Holy Spirit.

You didn't have to fill me up with more of Your Spirit,

But You did anyway.

So, Lord, I thank you

For being mindful of me today.

(Psalm 145:13, 18; Deuteronomy 31:8; Philippians 4:7)

My Daily Bread

I hunger and thirst for it.

For, apart from it,

I won't be, can't be, and will never be.

Who can live without it?

Who can walk right without it?

My daily bread is what I need

To live a life that is pleasing to You.

My daily bread is the very thing I need

To become all You created me to be.

My daily bread is what I look forward

To reading each day

And receiving each day.

So, Lord, thank you for my daily bread,

Your very Word that is a lamp unto my feet

And a light on my path.

Your love I need

To have compassion for others.

Your wisdom I need

To know right from wrong.

Your understanding I need

To not pass judgment on anyone.

Your very peace I need

To be still and know that You are God.

Your knowledge I need

To walk according to Your ways.

Thank You, Lord, for my daily bread.

Who can live without it?

Your very mercy to forgive as you forgive,

And your very power to accomplish all You have called me
to do,

Thank you, Lord, for more of You in my life today.

(Psalm 46:10, 119:105; Matthew 6:11; Nehemiah 8:10; Ephesians 4:32)

Another Day

Thank you, Lord, for this day.

Yes, Lord, it is indeed another day

You have made for me to give You praise,

Another day to see Your kingdom come in my life,

Another day to see Your will be done in my life

On earth and as it is in heaven.

Thank you, Lord, for another day

To see Your glory manifest in my life once more,

Another day to experience all You have in store,

Another day to accomplish all You have called me to do,

Another day to bless Your name that is above all names.

So, Lord, I thank you for this day

To be the head and not the tail,

Another day to see a shift in my situation,

Another day to see new opportunity come my way

And new doors open up to me.

Thank you, Father, for this new day.

(Matthew 6:10; Philippians 2:9; Deuteronomy 28:13)

Through It All

It seems like yesterday

When I counted the cost to follow You.

It was yesterday

When I confessed with my mouth that You are Lord,

And You've washed all my sins away

And forgiven me for all my sins.

It wasn't long ago

When I begin a new journey with You,

Not knowing where it was going to take me.

It was a journey

That started full of surprises

With many ups and downs,

Trials and tribulations,

Battles and victories,

Joys and sorrows.

It was a journey

That could either make me or break me,

But, by your grace,

It didn't break me.

I wondered if You had showed me everything

I was going to experience,

If I would have followed you.

You know them very well—

The setbacks, headaches, pain, trials, sufferings.

I wonder if You had said to me

That poverty, homelessness, and loneliness

Would still follow me for a while

If I would still count the cost and follow You.

Maybe not! Or maybe yes!

But one thing I can say for sure:

I'm glad You didn't reveal any details

But Your Word that says,

"I have plans to prosper you, not harm you,

Plans to give you hope and a future."

Because if You did,

I would not be the devoted woman I am today,

The woman of unshakable faith I am today.

I wouldn't know what Your restoration, healing,

Deliverance power feels like.

I wouldn't experience Your greatness

Or Your faithfulness in my life.

Thank You for the two decades of walking with You

And still standing tall

Through it all.

(Jeremiah 29:11)

Grace and Restoration

It Could Have Been a Lot Worse

In Awe

Again and Again

I Can Handle It

They Will Bow Down

I Look Forward, O Lord

They Didn't See It Coming

Just Been Set Free

I'm Grateful

This Is the Day

He's Worthy

All Things New

It Could Have Been a Lot Worse

How many are my kind who slept under the tunnel

In the cold weather last night?

And yet, You've blessed me with a warm place to stay.

Though I don't have a bed that I can call my own,

I'm blessed,

For it could have been a lot worse.

Really, who am I, Lord,

For whom you've always seemed to make a way out of no way?

Am I not one of them?

You overshadowed me day and night with Your favor.

Where I woke, others are opening their doors for me.

Who am I, Lord,

Who still has my praise with everything that's going on?

I am no different than they?

I will yet count my blessings,

For when I look at others' life struggles,

I see that it could have been a lot worse for me,

But Your grace was more than I could ask for.

Truly, Lord, Your breath of life is the very thing I need

To continue to bless Your name.

You have blessed me with a warm place with electricity

In which I can listen to some praise and worship songs.

Your presence is what I need to make my day.

Thank you, Lord, for Your grace.

It could have been a lot worse.

I could have woken up under the tunnel this morning.

In Awe

What can I say, Lord,

When each time I look

And all I see is Your favor

Surrounding me like a shield?

What can I say

When each time I look

And all I see around me

Is Your grace that is sufficient for me?

I am not where I used to be.

My face is no longer covered with shame.

Instead, I look more radiant than ever.

You have given beauty for ashes

And joy for mourning.

You delivered me from bondage,

Captivity, and lack.

At one point I thought I was doomed,

And You came and rescued me.

There's nothing else I can say.

Besides, I'm in awe.

I am in awe of Your goodness in my life.

I am in awe of Your faithfulness

That continues to shine upon me day and night.

I am in awe of Your grace

That is sufficient for me,

Your power that is in me

And is greater than any other power.

I am in awe of Your divine favor upon me

Where I see that I am blessed coming in

And blessed going out.

What more can I say

When each time I look,

All I see is Your glory, faithfulness, mercy, love, favor

Shining upon me like the stars?

Yes, Lord, I'm in awe of Your goodness.

You are, indeed, an awesome God

Thank you, great and awesome God

For Your goodness in my life.

(Psalm 5:12; 2 Corinthians 12:9; Isaiah 61:3; 1 John 4:4; Deuteronomy 28:6)

Again and Again

I try to explain it,

But I can't.

I try to understand it,

But I can't seem to comprehend it.

Again and again,

You kept blowing my mind

With Your goodness.

For once I am speechless.

There's no word to describe

How You've been good to me.

There's no word to describe

How You favor me.

Is there a place I go that I am not

Blessed coming in and blessed going out?

Is there a day that went by

When You didn't make a way for me?

Is there someone I met

That I did not find favor with?

For whatever reason,

Your glory can't stop shining upon me,

Doors can't seem to stay closed,

Situations can't seem to stay still,

People can't seem to let their no be no.

Whenever they said, "No,"

Suddenly you say, "Yes."

Really, Lord, who am I

That every day I'm seeing new favor,

Encounter, and mercy?

Who am I that Your glory

Can't stop shining upon me?

Again and again,

You keep on doing new things,

You keep on causing me to triumph.

I thought, could it be favoritism?

No, it cannot be favoritism,

For you are not a God of favoritism,

For if You do it for me,

You will do it for others.

It's nothing else but Your grace.

(2 Corinthians 12:9)

I Can Handle It

You don't have to worry about me.

You don't have to act all strange around me.

Relax, He did not forsake me.

He did not abandon me.

This is not the first time.

This is not a surprise to me.

I've been there multiple times,

And I've seen it all.

For I know what it's like to see other's prayers answered.

I know what it's like to see others living their dreams.

I know what it's like to see others living their full potential.

I know what it's like to see others climbing the ladder.

You don't have to worry about me.

You don't have to act all strange around me.

Relax, He did not forget about me.

He did not single me out.

I've been there multiple times.

I've seen it happen before.

Hear me out—you're not the only one with one.

Way before He blessed you,

He had already blessed me with mine.

I am also blessed—

Not with the typical blessings

You and I are accustomed to,

But with one that is invisible,

That no human can do anything to earn;

A blessing no one deserves.

It's a special grace to handle other's blessings,

To rejoice when they are rejoicing,

To celebrate them when their dreams come to pass,

To praise God for His goodness in their lives.

I understand not everyone can handle other's blessings,

I understand not everyone can rejoice when others are rejoicing,

But trust me when I say I can handle it.

So, you don't have to worry about me.

You don't have to act all strange around me.

I can handle it!

Yes, I can handle it

And have the grace to handle yours

With His grace, which is sufficient for me.

Thank you, Lord, for Your grace

To handle others' blessings.

(2 Corinthians 12:9)

They Will Bow Down

It will not be long.

It will not be long when they will soon see

Your mighty hands at work in my life,

When they will soon discover

There is one greater on the inside of me,

And when they will soon see

Your glory manifesting itself in my life.

O, how I believe!

How I believe, very soon,

They are going to know Your name,

The greatest name of all,

Whose daughter I am

And who fathered me.

It will not be long when they will soon discover

Who resides on the inside of me.

For once they are going to acknowledge your name,

For once they are going to know

I was never an accident,

I was never forsaken,

I was never abandoned,

I was never alone,

I was never out of my mind,

For once they are going to know

That my worship was never in vain.

O, how I believe!

How I believe it will not be long

When they will soon know

There was one always with me,

One always by my side,

One always for me,

One always working behind the scene.

All along there was one

Orchestrating things for me.

O, there was one

Who was with me and on my side.

So, thank you, Lord

For what you're getting ready to do for me.

Thank you, Lord

For how You're getting ready to reveal Yourself to man

And blow their minds.

For once they are going to bow down before You.

Never again will they bow down before other gods and worship them.

Never again will they serve two masters.

Never again will they call out on any other names.

Never again will they doubt Your ability and power.

Never again will they judge and slander me.

Indeed, Hallelujah, they won't have any choice,

But to bow down and worship You,

Bow down and glorify Your name,

Bow down and exalt You,

Bow down and magnify Your name.

Truly, they will bow down and worship.

Truly, they will bow down and glorify Your name.

Truly, they will bow down and exalt You.

They will worship you with all their minds,

With all their hearts,

And with all their strength.

They will bow down and worship You

Forever and ever.

(Exodus 34:14; 20:3; Luke 4:8; Matthew 6:24; James 4:11)

I Look Forward, O Lord

I look forward, O Lord, to seeing You

Make a way out of no way for me today.

Exercise Your power in my life,

To bring food to my table in a way I would never think or

imagine.

Yes, Lord, let Your glory be revealed in my life today,

For I look forward to testifying about Your glory.

I look forward, O Lord, to seeing You

Get me out of this poverty lifestyle,

Bring change to my condition

And restore my life.

Take me from faith to faith and glory to glory,

Demonstrate Your power in my life,

Open up the windows of heaven,

Pour out Your blessings in my life

And make a way for me in the wilderness.

Yes, Lord, I look forward, O Lord,
To seeing Your wonders manifest themselves in this famine
That I may proclaim Your good.

I look forward, O Lord,
To seeing Your glory manifest in a greater, higher, deeper
way in my life.
Today, Lord, I look forward
To seeing Your faithfulness shine upon me on this day.
Yes, Lord, Your daughter is looking forward
To seeing You change my condition for Your glory,
That men will know You are the God who supplies all Your
children's needs.
So, I look forward, O Lord, to seeing Your name
Glorified, magnified, and praised in my life.

They Didn't See It Coming

Many didn't believe

This day would actually come.

Many did not see this day coming

When God would restore my life,

When I would get up and dress to go work again.

Many didn't think this day was possible

When I would talk about my day at work.

Many didn't think it was possible

To get out of my situation some day.

Some even thought I was doomed

And there was no way out for me.

Many didn't believe that one day

I would experience a breakthrough—

Have a paycheck to go about my business.

Some thought I would never rise from the ashes.

Little did they know

God had a set time for me to be set free,

God had a set time for me to be delivered.

Surely, they did not see it coming, but God.

They forgot I serve a God

Who is not limited by any condition.

They forgot I serve a God

Who is the God of ancient days,

The God who delivered the Israelites from slavery

And made a way for them.

They forgot I serve a God

Who works behind the scenes,

Turning my situation around for me.

They did not see it coming,

But God saw it coming.

They did not see it coming,

But I saw it coming

Through the eyes of faith.

They did not see it coming,

But God saw it coming,

For He has made everything beautiful

In its time.

(Ecclesiastes 3:11)

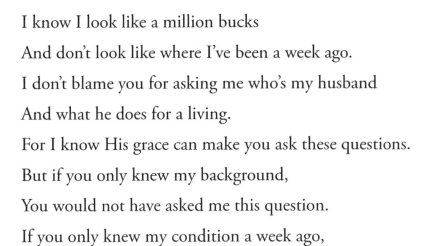

Just Been Set Free

I know I look like a million bucks

And don't look like where I've been a week ago.

I don't blame you for asking me who's my husband

And what he does for a living.

For I know His grace can make you ask these questions.

But if you only knew my background,

You would not have asked me this question.

If you only knew my condition a week ago,

You would not have been compelled to ask me this question.

You said to let you know

When I was having a yard sale,

But it was just a week ago

When I visited one,

Looking for something I could afford.

You said to think of you when I was having one,

But it was just recently

When I prayed,

Asking God to place me on someone's heart

To be a blessing to me.

I know I don't look like where I've been a week ago,

And in your eyes I look like a million bucks.

But if you only knew my past,

You would not have asked me those questions.

If you only knew where I've been the past several years,

You would not have asked me these questions.

It was just a week ago

When I was locked in a cage for half a decade

And waiting to be set free.

It was just a month ago

When I was collecting coins to get by.

It wasn't long ago

When I covered my head

For others not to see me

In the condition I was in.

Please don't be fooled by the fine clothes

And thinking I have some kind of wealth

Or a husband making six figures.

It's just His grace

That made you see millions

When I'd just been set free a week ago.

It's just His grace

That made you question me

About my husband.

In case you don't know,

The chains had fallen off of me just a week ago.

I had just been set free from below-poverty level.

I had just been set free from lack and shame.

I had just been set free from being a burden to loved ones.

It's not what you think.

In fact, you are in a better place in life than me.

For you have a place to call home, and I don't.

You have a vehicle you refuse to drive, and I don't.

You have one to keep you warm at night, and I don't.

So, don't be fooled by my fine clothes.

I had just been set free a week ago.

I'm Grateful

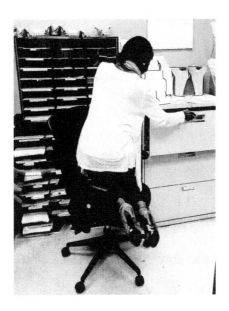

It may not be what you and I had hoped for all along,

But I'm grateful.

It may not be the desire of my heart,

But I'm grateful.

It may not be my dream job,

It may not be what I had been praying for,
But I'm grateful.
I'm grateful, I'm grateful, I'm grateful!

For I once was without one,
But now I have one.
I once couldn't move around,
But now I can.
I once was feeling shamed and embarrassed,
But now I feel powerful.
Now I don't have to cover my head to disguise myself
After being in bondage without a job for some time.
All I can say is, I'm grateful.
After being a slave to poverty,
All I can say is, I'm grateful.

It may not be the six-figure job you yourself have.
It may not be my type of environment.
It may not be as big as I had hoped.
I may be living paycheck to paycheck,
But I'm grateful.

For I was once in prison,

But now I'm free.

I once couldn't drive,

But now I can.

No, I did not settle for less.

I'm just grateful for the smallest thing—

For this door God has opened for me.

This Is the Day

You don't have to say more.

I will indeed rejoice and be glad in it.

Yes, on this day,

I will bless Him and magnify the Lord.

I will exalt Him, too,

For He has been good to me.

This is the day the Lord has made.

I will proclaim what He has done for me,

How He set me free

From homelessness, shame,

Humiliation, and rejection

And how He restored me

To the way I was before.

This is the day the Lord has made.

I will testify about His goodness in my life,

For I am no longer the needy,

I am no longer on the couch,

I am no longer occupying someone's bed.

The Lord has given us victory over our enemies

And caused judges to rule on our behalf.

I was bound in chains,

But the Lord set me free and delivered me.

I was about to lose my mind,

But the Lord kept it in peace.

This is the day the Lord has made.

I will rejoice and bless His name,

For no storm was too great for Him,

No chain was too strong for Him,

No enemy was too powerful for Him.

Day and night I will boast

Of His power of deliverance.

And yes, I will rejoice and be glad

On this very day,

For this is the day the Lord has made.

(Psalm 118:17; 24; Deuteronomy 20:4)

He's Worthy!

Believe it or not, I checked all the requirements,

And I did not find anyone who met them.

I did the background check,

But none came back positive.

I checked the references.

Unfortunately, there was no good feedback.

The weaknesses outnumbered the strengths,

And their history said it all.

Indeed, no one is eligible or qualified

To receive this very praise.

No one is trustworthy and faithful

To all of their promises

No one out there can deliver me

Or set me free like He did.

I called over and over—

No one came to my rescue.

Everyone turned their backs against me.

I was left alone

With my back against the wall.

I was left alone

With no one to come to my rescue.

Truly, my God is worthy of this praise.

No one qualifies or is worthy of it

But my Father, who is my rock,

My deliverer, my provider, and my healer.

I was in great distress,

And no one came to help,

But it was He who stood by my side

Throughout the entire time.

Before I called for help,

He was already present,

Not in ways I had hoped,

But in ways He knows were best.

It was He who came to my rescue.

It was He who made a way out of no way.

It was He who did not leave my side.

He alone is worthy of all my praise.

Therefore, I will not give my praise to another

Nor bow down to worship anyone

But Him who is most worthy of praise,

And who restored my life.

(Psalm 18, 145:13)

All Things New

Yes, Lord! Yes, Lord! Yes, Lord!

Go ahead and have Your way in me.

Go ahead and do the new thing in me as You promised.

For You alone act when You speak

And fulfill when You promise.

So, I say, yes, Lord,

Do a new thing in me,

Have your way and do your thing,

For new is Your name,

Beginning is Your name,

Alpha is Your name,

First is Your name.

Therefore, I thank You for making all things new.

I thank You for where You're getting ready to take me.

I thank You for the new season of change,

The new ideas, concepts, knowledge,
Understanding, and revelations I will receive.

Yes, Lord, Yes, Lord, have Your way in me!
May Your Glory be revealed in my life
While You make all things new.
May Your name be praised in my life
While You do a new thing in me.
And may Your name be exalted in my life
While You take me to a new level in You.
Thank You for new provisions and opportunities
That are coming my way today
And for making all things new!

(Isaiah 43:19; Numbers 23:19)

Goodbye Boston, Massachusetts

And Hello Iowa, USA

Thank You, Lord, for restoring my life!

"Now faith is confidence in what we hope for
and assurance about what we do not see."

—Hebrews 11:1 (NIV)

About the Author

Myrlande Joseph is a devoted, anointed woman of God with a heart of worship. She is also a multi-gifted, multi-talented woman who loves to bless the Lord in the midst of her storms and has inspired many of her friends and family to do the same.

Myrlande is a worshiper, a prayer warrior, a solo praise dancer, a servant leader, an inspirational writer, and a speaker who always has a word of encouragement and wisdom for others. She is called to serve the poor and needy and to share God's goodness around the world. In 1996, at age twenty, she received Jesus Christ as her Lord and Savior, and she has not stopped walking with Him since. She loves the Lord!

Myrlande holds a B.A. in Management from Eastern Nazarene College in Quincy, Massachusetts, and an M.S. in Nonprofit Management and Leadership from Northeastern University in Boston. Over the last nineteen years she has served in different ministries in such capacities as record-keeping, intercessor, praise and worship team member, greeter, children's ministry worker, and usher. She has also used her solo praise dance ministry to lead Sunday morning worship at local churches, conferences, and other annual events.

Writing about God, testifying on His behalf, praising Him, and serving the poor are her greatest loves. Writing is the medium through which she feels most free to express her deepest thoughts and feelings. It is also where she finds peace and trust in God during whatever trial she is experiencing. From her experience, it is through praise and worship that God reveals Himself to her. Myrlande hopes, by sharing her unique poems, that she will not only positively affect other people's lives but will also draw them nearer to God.

This is Myrlande's third book. In 2008, while unemployed for some time, the Lord charged her to send out daily words of encouragement via group emails, through which many were blessed. After several years of this, in 2014, she completed her first book, *An Ordinary Girl*, her autobiography, as well as another spiritually inspirational title, *Don't Be Afraid To Pray*. She is now on a journey to publish them so that she can testify about the power of prayer and share how she discovered God's purpose for her journey. In addition, she will soon launch a praise blog, unstoppablepraise.com, which she is designing to encourage and inspire others to bless the Lord at all times. She hopes to publish other spiritually inspirational books and poetry albums in the near future.

Made in the USA
Middletown, DE
13 September 2020